IND

CW00508839

Celebrating the History of
Southampton Hospital Radio

The first 50 years
1952 to 2002
by Roy Stubbs

Published by
PALMA PUBLICATIONS
268a Priory Road
Southampton
SO17 2LS

Southampton Hospital Broadcasting Association
The Studio Centre
Tebourba Way
Southampton
SO16 4QE

Registered Charity No. 259459

Typeset by Acanthus
Printed by Ashford Press
Bound by Itchen Press Ltd

ISBN   Number
0-9542350-0-2

Celebrating the History of

Southampton Hospital Radio

1952-2002

with

Roy Stubbs

Dedicated to all members, past and present, whose tireless enthusiasm has made Southampton Hospital Radio the great organisation that it is today.

The official registered name of the charity is Southampton Hospital Broadcasting Association. However we are better known as "Southampton Hospital Radio" - or just, "Hospital Radio" and for the past 50 years our members have been using the acronym "HBA"

Unfortunately in 1993, NAHBO (The National Association of Hospital Broadcasting Organisations) decided to adopt, for their own trading purposes, the acronym "HBA"

We objected but lost the cause. Throughout this book the letters HBA always refer to the Southampton Association.

NAHBO has remained with its name unchanged

Introduction

1952 to 2002

To celebrate our 50th Anniversary Year I have been privileged to put together this book for the benefit of the members of HBA. I have only been a member for 21 years, so the earlier years have been researched from files of minutes, programmes, newsletters and many long conversations with some of the "old timers".

At the Southern Daily Echo archives, I was allowed to read not only the Daily Echo of 18th October 1952, but also study the "Pink" Football Echo of the same date, detailing the results of the football match where our history all began. I was also allowed to select some of the pictures that have appeared in the press over the years.

To compress 50 years of history into but a few chapters means that I have omitted vast quantities of events, stories and pleasurable memories. I apologise if your particular memorable event has not been included, and sincerely apologise to the dozens of former members whose names may have been omitted. You have not been forgotten by the patients who enjoyed your programme whilst they were in hospital, nor by your family and friends who all envied your membership in a club that only the privileged few were allowed to join.

So let's go back in time to when it all began . . . . . .

We were not the first hospital radio station. There were a few others broadcasting football commentaries way back in the mid 1930's. However our history began with the first football commentary from The Dell when Saints played Doncaster Rovers on 18th October 1952.

The Music Section was formed in March 1963 to play record requests. These programmes were initially recorded on reels of tape and then played through the Southampton Rediffusion radio network. The first live music programme was broadcast from our Toc H Cellar Studio on 2nd January 1966.

The broadcasting studio was in the basement of their Building at the top of the Avenue. Later Toc H gave us a lease on a part of their garden, where we constructed our first real radio studio. The first broadcast "above ground" in our second studio was on 1st August 1971 and this studio was officially opened by Earl Mountbatten on 12th October 1971.

In 1978 we were advised that our site was required by developers and a new studio was then built on a plot of land in the grounds of the Chest Hospital. A 21 year lease from January 1981 was granted by the Hospital Authorities. However it took three years of hard labour to raise the funds and to build and fit out this, our third new studio. The opening ceremony and the first programme was broadcast by Lord and Lady Romsey on 11th December 1981.

This building of brick and tiles was meant to last forever, but Tesco came along and persuaded us to move once again. Our studio was located where they wanted to put their store entrance roadway, so we moved, just 100 yards along the road into a magnificent new studio. Funds for this move were provided by Tesco and Danny LaRue opened this, our fourth home, on 12th December 1993.

A new 21 year lease on this piece of land, still at the peppercorn rent of £1 per annum was granted by the Hospital Authorities on 13th December 1993, and we hope to be here for evermore.

Originally Toc H Hospital Broadcasting but when we registered as a charity on 10th February 1970 we were known as "Hospital Broadcasting Association (Southampton and Winchester)". Our name and Constitution was later changed in March 1991 to "Southampton Hospital Broadcasting Association". However we have always been affectionately known as both "HBA" and "Southampton Hospital Radio".

CHAPTER 1

Football

1952 to 1963

Leslie Arthur Sullivan joined Toc H around 1930 and in 1933, at the age of 26 he started a Toc H branch in Barnstaple. At that time there was not a national blood transfusion service and Toc H started this service by finding blood donors for the local hospital. This, however, was only a small part of Leslie's good works.

With another Toc H member he also visited the casualty wards at Barnstaple Hospital on Sunday afternoons, taking with him a record player and records, organising a sing-song for the "gentlemen of the road" who seemed to congregate there. (The start of hospital radio requests!)

In 1939 he arranged to take over a disused Church Army Hall in Plymouth as a canteen for servicemen. This was financed by collecting waste paper, an acquired fund-raising skill he was to put to good use later in his lifetime, to help HBA.

As Leslie was not considered medically fit for national service he joined the Home Guard and put in command of a gun battery during the war defending Plymouth at Mount Edgecombe.

With two other Toc H members he also organised and helped run an all night Rest House outside the Plymouth railway station. This was set-up to meet the needs of the travelling servicemen and their families en route to the West Country who were regularly left stranded overnight. They provided an all-night service of teas and snacks as well as a bed. Their first house was bombed, but then later found another and ended up with two joined together offering 80 beds - all provided free by Toc H.

The name Toc H is derived from the telegraphic signallers shortening for "Talbot House" which is the name given to their headquarters building.

In 1945 when the all-night Rest Home closed, he did his first broadcast for the BBC recounting his wartime adventures.

This led to him broadcasting regularly on BBC as a freelance reporter doing local news items - the start of his broadcasting career.

In 1946 Leslie was going to watch Plymouth Argyle play their first evening match since their football stand had been burned down during the blitz. Jim, the switchboard operator at his firm, who had been blinded at Anzio, said he would love to go, so Leslie took him on his arm and they stood together in the crowd with Leslie giving a running commentary.

With the help of Len Collier, a local schoolteacher, he then arranged for a bench on the touchline for themselves and four blind supporters and continued with this commentary, also recording it onto tape.

This recording was later played to the patients in Plymouth hospital, fully supported by the football club who supplied the bench and free passes to their special visitors.

Leslie returned to Southampton in 1948 and later heard that Toc H had started a Hospital Radio football service in Bristol, using their local Rediffusion service.

Aware that Rediffusion were also operating here, he set about trying to organise a similar system for the Southampton hospitals, but instead of recording onto a portable tape recorder he went one better and arranged a live commentary direct from The Dell to the Rediffusion Centre. He arranged for a GPO telephone line to be installed at the Dell connected permanently to the Rediffusion centre in Lyon Street. His commentary was then transmitted along the Rediffusion network to the General and the Royal South Hants Hospitals and then later also to the Chest Hospital.

At the start of the football project Leslie wrote numerous letters seeking financial support and received two cheques. The first for £10.00 came from Earl Mountbatten and the second for £5.00 was from Carey & Lambert, the local Car Sales firm at Stag Gates.

The annual charges of £75.00 for the GPO landline, plus a fee payable to

Rediffusion of two guineas each match for the hire of the microphones, mixer and amplifiers were then taken on board.

With liabilities of over £100.00, and with only £15 in the bank, Leslie Sullivan took the plunge and started the service.

To consider the size of this project, as a comparison, Ken's Flood's take home pay was around £9.00 per week and the price of a new three bedroomed house was about £1,500. A £100 commitment was quite significant at that time. Ken's wife remembers that their daily food budget was 2/6d (about 12 pence in today's money)

After paying the costs relating to the commentaries for the first two home matches, the Southampton Football Club then took responsibility for the GPO line and Rediffusion hire charges, and HBA was now in business. The Football Club used funds from the Charity Match, held at the beginning of each season, to meet our financial needs.

The GPO line charges were initially for the RSH and the General but as other hospitals were added to the network so these charges increased. The Rediffusion equipment hire charges continued at the same level, but these were eventually waived altogether in 1960.

The Southampton football match on 18th October 1952 when Saints played Doncaster Rovers, was our first live broadcast and the three commentators were Leslie Sullivan, N. K. Bean (Inky), the warden of the Toc H Seafaring Boys Residential Hostel, and Frank Le Druillenec.

The ten minute interval at half time was filled by the commentators setting a quiz for the patients and the answers were sent, by postcard, back to HBA. The winners were then presented with their prizes by a footballer visiting the wards.

Our first away game was in 1958 when Saints played at Norwich and, by using a telephone line, we broadcast the commentary provided by Norwich Hospital Radio to the Southampton Hospital patients.

In 1955 at the age of 25 Ken Flood, a keen footballer and manager of the Southampton University Staff Association Football Club when playing for his team, caught a ball in the eye and was forced to lie on his back, for a week, in the Southampton Eye Hospital. On the Wednesday evening the Hospital Radio football commentary from the Dell was his first introduction to a hobby that would remain with him for ever.

As a qualified Radio and TV engineer, for financial reasons he moved in 1958 from his job at Southampton University to go to work for Rediffusion, the Southampton cabled wireless company.

After a couple of months, because he was a keen football enthusiast, he was offered the job, at Saturday overtime rates, to connect the switches on the Hospital Radio broadcasting system. This meant going to the Dell in the morning and setting up the Vortexion mixer and the two microphones. Then, by leaving the sound effects microphone switched on, as a sound test, he would drive to the RSH, the General, the Chest Hospital and the Eye Hospital to switch on the hospital amplifiers.

In the afternoon he would go to the match, sit on the steps alongside the three HBA commentators with his headset on, and operate the sound mixer. The commentators had three seats in the front row of the West Stand, didn't wear headphones, and passed the one hand-held microphone between them, leaving the background sound effects microphone hanging over the edge of the balcony.

Mixing the commentators sound was quite a skill, which Ken honed with lots of practice. At the end of the match he would then return the mixer and microphones to the Rediffusion workshop and travel around all four Hospitals once again to switch off the connections.

Evening matches meant the task sometimes wasn't finished until way past 10.30pm. It was a tough job, being paid at time and a half overtime rates, to watch the Saints, but someone had to do it.

In 1960 when Inky Bean died, Ken was offered one of the HBA commentating seats and so he moved from the steps and took up a proper seat, but still continued to operate the mixer, and also assisted with the commentating. He still operates the mixer from his seat 42 years on.

The Southampton Football Echo on Saturday 18th October 1952, with the result of the match. The headline reads "Frank Dudley playing a dashing game, scored a "hat-trick" in the first half hour". With six goals in the match it probably made Sully's commentary pretty enjoyable.
(Photograph courtesy of Southampton Daily Echo)

Arthur Leslie "Sully" Sullivan sat in the West Stand at The Dell and broadcast the whole of the historic match on October 18th 1952. (Photograph courtesy of Southampton Daily Echo)

On the air this week-end

WEST
(285m. and 206m.). — 5, Children. 5.55, Weather. 6, News. 6.15, Sport in the West. 6.40, At the Luscombes. 7, In Town Tonight. 7.30, Week in Westminster. 7.45, Star Show. 9, News. 9.15, Theatre: " Love in Idleness." 10.45, Prayers. 11, News.

SUNDAY
7.50 a.m., Reading. 7.55, Weather. 8, News. 8.20, Concert Orchestra. 9.5, Regional Weather Forecast. 9.8, Week in the West. 9.30, Service. 10.15, Promenade Records. 11.15, Portrait Sketch. 11.30, Music Magazine. 12.10 p.m., The Critics. 12.55, Weather. 1, News. 1.10, Country Questions. 1.40, Two Pianos. 2, For Western Gardeners. 2.15, West Country Diary. 2.30, " Oranges and Lemons " (Phillip Wade). 3.45, BBC Concert Orchestra. 4.45, Books. 5, Children. 5.50, Money Matters. 5.55, Weather. 6, News. 6.15, UN Assembly. 6.30, BBC Symphony Concert. 7.45, Service. 8.30, " Mansfield Park " (No. 7). 9, News. 9.15, King George VI Memorial Fund. 9.20, " The Guv'nor " (tribute to George Edwardes). 10.20, Kyla Greenbaum (piano). 10.52, Epilogue. 11, News.

HOME
(330m.) — 5, Children. 5.55, Weather. 6, News. 6.15, Sport. 6.30, Harry Davidson Orchestra. 7-11, See West.

SUNDAY
7.50 a.m. - 1.40 p.m., See West. 1.40, Opera Records. 2, Home Grown. 2.30-11, See West.

LIGHT
(1.500m. and 247m.). — 5.30, Sports Report. 6, Jane Froman (records). 6.15, " Just William." 6.45, Can I Help You?: Dudley Perkins. 7, News; Newsreel. 7.25, Sport. 7.30, The Archers. 8.30, Family Favourites. 9.15, Handel's " Messiah." Part 2: Jennifer Vyvyan (soprano), William Herbert (tenor), Richard Standen (bass); Choir; L.S.O. 10, News. 10.15, Show Band. 11, Jack Jackson's Record Round-up. 11.56-12, News.

SUNDAY
8 a.m., Variety Orchestra. 8.30, Stanley Black Dance Orchestra. 9, News. 9.10, Today's Job: Bernard Wetherall. 9.15, Hullo There! (for young listeners). 10, Royal Artillery (Woolwich) Band. 10.30, Countryside songs: Jan van der Gucht (tenor), Robert Irwin (baritone), BBC (men) Singers. 11, Sid Phillips' Band. 11.30, Service. 12, Family Favourites. 1.15, Billy Cotton Band Show. 1.45, " Educating Archie " (repeat). 2.15, Songs for You: David Hughes. 2.45, Henry Hall's Guest Night. 3.30, Down Your Way." 4.30, " The Regent " (serial play). 5, Book by the Fire: Alan Melville. 5.30, Disc-Doodling: Flotsam. 6, Round Britain Quiz: London v. North Region. 6.30, " Double Top ": Anne Shelton. Alfred Marks. 7, News. Newsreel. 7.30, " The Girl in the Dark ": BBC Repertory Company. 8.30, Community hymn-singing. 9, Tom Jenkins' Palm Court Orchestra. 10, News. 10.15, Charlie Kunz (piano). 10.30, Hymns. 10.45, Sandy Macpherson (organ). 11.15, Elton Hayes (guitar). Louis Stevens' Quintet. 11.35, Tom Jones Trio. 11.56-12, News.

THIRD
(464m. and 194m.).— 6 p.m., Scarlatti Sonatas: Clara Haskill (piano). 6.20, Cape Coloured Community: Sheila Patterson (talk). 6.45, " The Dead City " (play, repeat). 8, Concert, Part 1: Campoli (violin); BBC Symphony Orchestra. 8.45, Counter-Revolution of Science: Prof. J. W. N. Watkins (talk). 9.5, Concert, continued. 9.50, Meditation for St. Luke's Day: Canon F. L. Hilditch. 10.5, Grelg: Randi Helseth (soprano), Iris Loveridge (piano). 10.55, Foreign Review (repeat). 11.25-11.50, Robert Lowell (poems, repeat).

SUNDAY
6 p.m., " Gotterdammerung," Act 1. 8, An Un-English Activity?—Prof. Nikolaus Pevsner (talk). 8.25, "A Company of Fools": James Kirkup poems. 8.40, " Gotterdammerung." Act 2. 9.50, Law Reform: Prof. Glanville Williams. 10.10, " Gotterdammerung." Act 3. 11.30-11.50, Chasing a Phoenix (talk, repeat).

VISION
5-6 p.m., Children: SS " Saturday Special ": Capt. Peter Butterworth. 7.15, Week's Newsreels. 8.30, Looking at Animals: George Cansdale. 8.50, " Happy and Glorious," Episode 6: Renee Asherson. 9.25, Music-Hall, from Kodak Theatre, Harrow. 10.40, Weather; News.

SUNDAY
2.15-3.30 p.m., Duke of Gloucester presents Colours to 18th Bn. Parachute Regiment: F.-M. Viscount Montgomery; Service of Consecration: Rev. K. A. Puntan. 5-6, Children. 8, " Mr. Pim Passes By ": Mary Ellis, D. A. Clarke-Smith, Arthur Wontner (comedy). 9.25, What's My Line? 10.5, Organ Recital: George Thalben-Ball. 10.25, Weather, News.

The radio programmes reprinted from the Daily Echo of 18th October 1952.

The patients could chose between channels A, B or C - the Light, Home or Foreign. The Home switched to the "West programmes" in this area and HBA used channel C whenever we were on air.

Some really old radio favourites can be recalled including:- The Archers, Family Favourites, Jack Jackson's Record Roundup, The Stanley Black Dance Orchestra, Sid Phillips' Band, Billy Cotton Band Show, Educating Archie, Henry Hall's Guest Night, Down Your Way and Round Britain Quiz.

(Photograph courtesy of Southampton Daily Echo)

CHAPTER 2
The Music Section
1963 to 1964

In 1962 John Stranger, a young man of 21, from Guernsey, was lodging at the Toc H Mark V Hostel, Winchester Road, Bassett, and following a short stay in the Royal South Hants Hospital, complained that he could not hear the football commentary, so he investigated how the hospital football broadcasting system worked. On his return to Toc H he contacted Leslie Sullivan, who was on the board, and was informed that we did not broadcast the Saints Charity Match. John was then astounded to hear that we were renting a telephone line for 365 days of the year, but using it only on the days when the Saints were playing. He made enquiries around his Toc H contacts and heard that Bristol, being one step ahead of us again, had started playing record requests to their listeners, so he went about forming a "Music Section".

On 21st March 1963 he called the first meeting of the Hospital Broadcasting Music Committee, the object being to elect a committee who would supervise the running of the Southampton Hospitals Record request programmes.

At this inaugural meeting along with John Stranger were Ken Flood, Fred Booker, Charles Heseltine, Brian Exon, Ian Mackenzie-Williams and Bill Tanner.

Bill Tanner, the general manager at Rediffusion, who came from Bristol, already knew of the Hospital Radio music programmes that were broadcasting on the Bristol Rediffusion network and allowed the group to use his office for their initial meetings.

Following articles in the local newspaper and the distribution of request cards around the hospitals, John collected record requests and also received a few donated records. From his accommodation at Toc H, John then produced the first three or four weekly taped request programmes.

The first tape he made ran for one hour and twenty-nine minutes with about

100 requests, and when Rediffusion broadcast the tape they simply left it to run its full length.

As there was only one tape in use, the later programmes, which were not so long, then left a "tail" of the previous recordings. As Rediffusion never stopped the tape, this did cause some problems with the tail end requests being repeated.

These recordings were not very high in the quality department so Ken Flood arranged for Bill Tanner's office to be set-up as a recording studio on a Tuesday afternoon. Ken Flood would get out the football section's Vortexion mixer and set up a tape-recording machine. Around 4.30pm. John would bring in the records and request cards after work, and with the aid of a Dansette Record Player, John and Ken would together make a music request tape.

After a few weeks this operation then moved to the chief engineer's office at Rediffusion, with Ken still operating the equipment and John doing the talking.

The tape, which normally ran for 45 minutes, was then carried downstairs to the Rediffusion operations room and the operator, inserting the output into the Rediffusion transmission network, broadcast it initially at 5.00pm every Wednesday.

As John Stranger was organising the request cards, collecting the records and doing the presenting he decided to hire a professional tape-recording machine and started the recording sessions back at Toc H using the "visitor's bedroom" where Tubby Clayton stayed whenever he visited the Hostel, with Ian Mackenzie-Williams operating the machinery.

The technical quality of the tapes however was still not very good.

Ken Flood continued with the football section and was also appointed as the first Secretary to the new music section. The minutes of the committee meetings during 1963 were prepared by Ken in his excellent handwriting. These early meetings were held in the Rediffusion offices, however, later on in 1963 the meetings were then being held at Toc H and Miss Maureen Houlihan joined the committee. Maureen took over the preparation of the minutes and her beautiful script followed in Ken's pattern, so that our historical records have been faithfully preserved.

Maureen, a young nurse at the Children's Hospital, was over here from Jersey and met John Stranger at the Children's Hospital's Christmas Dance in 1962. The Matron had contacted Toc H and invited "suitable young men" to attend. Four young men turned up and one of them proved to be eminently suitable, and they were married in October 1964

At the inaugural music section meeting on 21st March 1963 it was resolved to ask Leslie Sullivan, the founding member of the football section, who was also the chairman of Toc H at that time, to join the group.

Music requests would be broadcast to the four Hospitals currently receiving the football commentaries : The Chest, Eye, General and Royal South Hants and the taped programme would go out on a Wednesday evening between 5pm and 6pm in order not to clash with any football broadcasts.

Record request cards would be printed and placed in the Hospitals and patients would send these in the mail. 18 or 19 would be selected every Tuesday evening and a record request programme recorded.

On the 30th March 1963 Len Lucena and Mrs J Cunningham-Smith travelled down from the Bristol Hospital Radio and gave a talk at Toc H, Winchester Road, Southampton.

At the April meeting it was agreed, at that stage, not to merge the football and music request section funds, as the costs of the football section were being supported from the proceeds of the charity match at The Dell.

Borrowing records was not easy and many of the record shops in town had been approached and, following an article in the local paper, Mr Jefferey of Liberty Coin Ltd, offered his help. He had a turnover of 50,000 records per annum in his JukeBox machines and we could borrow his spares, but they were not "in any order". Ian Mackenzie - Williams and Mr Sullivan Junior volunteered to sort them and spent many evenings cataloguing his stock.

J & M Stone agreed to help by recording our list of music requests on to a tape for us, but this was not very successful as 45% of our requests were for older types of music - J & M Stone only had "pop" music in stock and patients were therefore not getting their musical requests.

Unfortunately, in July 1963, the tape-recorder which John was using at Toc H, on loan from the Technical College, had to be returned, but this was replaced by another loaned machine from the Civic Centre library. However in August, Southampton Group Hospital Management Committee agreed to fund the purchase of new recording equipment.

Another letter to the Southampton Echo seeking donations of "old" records, resulted in about 150 records for our library. The Echo also volunteered to advertise our request service, so the following was to be printed every Wednesday : "Toc H record request programme to Southampton Hospitals to-night 5 - 6pm"

In September, suggestions for a short talk by the Hospital Chaplains should be added at the end of each request programme. This was agreed in principle, but proved to be difficult to achieve with the taped music programmes. However, it was later introduced when programmes went live.

John's team continued to progress and Don Moxon, the Toc H warden joined the committee and gave permission for us to use the Toc H premises, not only as a regular meeting place, but also as a mailing address. The first committee meeting was held there at our first "home" on 24th October 1963.

A letter of thanks was sent to Mrs Williams at J & M Stone, who had taped our requests each week in her shop. They were discontinuing their record section and were no longer able to help.

P.A.Baker came to our rescue and agreed to "loan" us a selection of their latest pop records. At that time, record shops had record-playing booths for customers to sample their 45 rpm records before making a purchase, so used 45's were not too unusual. John Stranger arranged to call in at 5.15 in the evening with a promise to return them at 9.15 the following morning "played once".

It had been suggested that we should tape every record and start our own tape library. However that was not considered practical as there would have been a serious storage and cataloguing problem. We knew that Bristol Hospital Radio only used 45's and they were all borrowed, so we continued to borrow records and started our own collection of donated records, mostly 78's, at this stage

Publishing patients' names and their request details in the Echo had proved to be embarrassing as one of the patients had died before the request had been played. The Echo was therefore no longer to be supplied with patients' names.

The record request postcards with our address pre-printed on the front were placed in the hospitals in boxes fixed to the walls and patients would drop them in the mail to us. Initially, 1500 cards were printed free of charge by Ellans Ltd, but this was quickly followed within a few months with a further print run of 5,000 cards. Complaints were received from one or two hospitals, stating that the record request card boxes were regularly empty. Topping-up these boxes was a major administrative problem and students from Taunton's School were drafted in to help.

Sometimes there were not enough request cards to fill a programme and Maureen Houlihan and Marjorie Sullivan would together call into the Hospital to collect requests from patients. (The start of our hospital visiting team.)

By January 1964, the Treasurer reported that funds in hand were £87.00 and it was agreed to purchase a portable tape-recorder for 18 guineas.

Also in January the Hospital Management Committee agreed to pay for the connection and running costs of a GPO line to The Fred Woolley Home of Recovery and our service was also extended to the Children's Hospital in Winchester Road. The GPO line connection charge to there was quoted as £2.00 plus a further £2.00 per annum for running costs.

It was also noted in the January minutes that Mrs Sullivan joined the team, keeping John Stranger's wife Maureen (Miss Houlihan at that time) company on the committee.

Performing Rights problems were clarified with the receipt of a letter of exemption dated 18th March 1964.

However in February 1964 two very significant events occurred:-

First:

The members of the committee who were meeting in the dining room at Toc H, adjourned to inspect the cellar. It had been estimated that repairs and renovation costs to make this habitable would be about £300 as this cellar was on the agenda to be considered as our first real home.

Second:

Geoff Allcock was elected as a member of the committee.

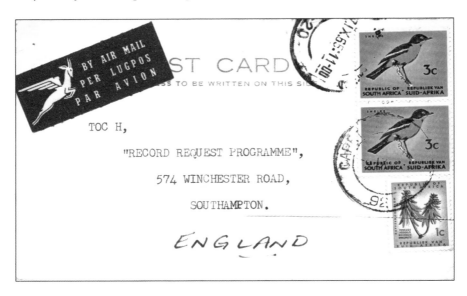

PATIENTS NAME *WILSON ROBERTSON* (Mr/~~Mrs~~/~~Miss~~)

WARD .... *K* .... HOSPITAL *CHEST, SOUTHAMPTON*

YOUR NAME *SHIRLEY CLIFFORD* (~~Mr~~/~~Mrs~~/Miss)

YOUR ADDRESS *P.O. BOX 1060, CAPE TOWN, SOUTH AFRICA*

EXPECTED DATE OF DISCHARGE *LATE NOVEMBER*

RELATIONSHIP TO PATIENT *FRIEND*

RECORD REQUESTED *SEPTEMBER SONG BY NAT KING COLE*
GEORGE SHEARING PLAYING

ANY SPECIAL MESSAGE *WITH ALL MY LOVE*

CARDS TO BE RETURNED MONDAYS. BROADCASTS WED. &
FRI. AT 5 P.M. BY ARRANGEMENT WITH REDIFFUSION &
SUPPORT OF BONHOMIE CLUB.

An example of a record request card sent in by listeners.

These were preprinted in thousands. Blanks were left in the hospital foyers and it was
sometimes difficult to keep the wall boxes regularly filled.

Toc H
December 1964
HOSPITAL BROADCASTS
Southampton

YOUR   OWN   SPECIAL   PROGRAMME

YOUR WEDNESDAY DISC JOCKEY
JOHN STRANGER
Responsible for the intro-
duction of musical progra-
mmes to the system in 1963
Occupation: Manager, soft
    drink manufacturers

YOUR FRIDAY DISC JOCKEY
ZENA MILLARD
Newest member of the HBS
Likes 'pop', traditional
jazz, loves Chris Barber
Occupation: Ladies' Hair
    dresser

REQUEST   PROGRAMMES
presented between 5 & 6 p.m.
each WEDNESDAY & FRIDAY.

THIS NEWS SHEET IS CIRCULATED TO ALL SOUTHAMPTON HOSPITALS BY THE KIND
PERMISSION OF THE SOUTHAMPTON HOSPITAL MANAGEMENT COMMITTEE

The first "Hospital Radio Times"
Page 1

CHIEF ENGINEER
GEOFF. ALLCOCK
Responsible for technical
facilities. Is also stand
in D.J. Likes light music
Occupation: Experimental
Officer

HEAD OUTSIDE BROADCASTS
JOHN GIBBONS
In charge of newly formed
team organised to deliver
the city to your bedside.
Occupation: Trainee Elec-
tronics Engineer

SPECIAL CHRISTMAS PROGRAMMES 1964

SATURDAY 19th DECEMBER — Southampton v Newcastle U. Football Match from the Dell commencing at 2.50p.m.

TUESDAY 22nd DECEMBER — SPECIAL CHRISTMAS PROGRAMME   5 - 6 p.m.
This programme will include a message to hospitals from the Mayor, the Right Worshipful Councillor E.E. Willcock; carols from children and from the boys of King Edward VI school. Their will be interviews with old people, a message from Father Christmas and a closing address by the Right Reverend the Lord Bishop of Southampton, Kenneth Lamplough

WEDNESDAY 23rd DECEMBER — Special Joint Disc Jockey Record Request prog.

SATURDAY 26th DECEMBER — Southampton v Plymouth Argyle Football Match from the Dell commencing at 2.50p.m.

MANY OF THE RECORDS PLAYED IN OUR REQUEST RECORD PROGRAMMES
ARE LOANED TO US BY P.A. BAKER, 111, ABOVE BAR, SOUTHAMPTON

The first "Hospital Radio Times"
Page 2

FOOTBALL COMMENTARIES

FOOTBALL COMMENTATOR
LESLIE SULLIVAN
Originator of Toc H football
broadcasts to hospitals over
eleven years ago   "Sully"
Occupation: Sales Manager

FOOTBALL COMMENTATOR
KEN FLOOD
Mad about football at school
(and since). Hibernates when
the "close" season's with us
Occupation: Electronics Tech
                           nician

FOOTBALL COMMENTATOR
FRANK LE DRUILLENEC
Another early commentator
who would not miss a game
if you're on the ball too
Occupation: Administrator

LIVE COMMENTARIES are brought
to you on all first team Home
matches from the Dell. Occasionally we relay a commentary
given by our colleagues else-
where on away matches and cup
ties.
You can hear Hospital Broadcasts by switching your headphone indicator to a position
which carries a foreign programme by day and Radio Luxembourg in the evening whenever
HBS is not "on the air".
If you have any difficulty in
receiving the programme owing
to low level or distorted qua
lity please attempt to let us
know as soon as possible. Our
telephone number is 68107.

✦   ✦   ✦   ✦   ✦   ✦

HOSPITAL BROADCAST PROGRAMMES ARE BROUGHT TO YOU WITH THE CO-OPERATION
OF REDIFFUSION LTD.

The first "Hospital Radio Times"
Page 3

Since last August, the staff of HBS has been hard at work converting the cellars under Toc H Mark V, Winchester Rd. into a fully equipped broadcasting studio.

We anticipate that work will be completed during March so that programmes which are at present taped may be transmitted live. Additional features will then include special programmes for the children and HBS will be "on the air" every night of the week with programmes designed for your enjoyment.

You would assist us greatly if you would write detailing the kind of programmes that you would wish to hear when lying in bed. We appreciate that the information is unlikely to benefit you since you will be discharged before we can inaugurate these ideas but it will enable us to plan features of special interest for those who follow you in the future.

Our address is as follows-
Southampton Hospital Broadcasts,
Toc H Mark V,
Winchester Road,
Bassett,
Southampton.
THANK YOU

+ + + + + + + + + + + +   + +   + + + + + + + + + +

ACKNOWLEDGEMENTS

The Hospitals Broadcasting System could not exist without the generous assistance offered to us by the Southampton Football Club and we have pleasure in acknowledging this assistance and to thank them for their appreciation of our aims.

+ + + + + + + +

PLEASE HELP US

Please tell your ward mates especially the newcomers how to receive our transmissions If there is a headphone shortage please request these of Sister. In cases of shortage or difficulty write or telephone us at Toc H.

INCIDENTALLY

It costs you 2½d (the price of the stamp) to have a request played over HBS.

It costs Toc H considerably more than this. Where do we obtain our funds?

We rely in the main on voluntary contributions and so if you would like to assist please send your contribution -no matter how large or small- to us at the address given. We shall be most grateful.

+ + + + + + + + +

There are many people behind the scenes, too many to mention individually who voluntarily give their assistance to make your programme possible. We know that you would wish to offer them greetings this Christmas.

The first "Hospital Radio Times"
Page 4

CHAPTER 3

Taped Programmes
1963 to 1966

Ken Flood, aware of the lack of technical expertise within the HBA team asked his friend Geoff Allcock, if he would be interested in helping out.

When Ken was working at Southampton University he had worked with Geoff, who served his apprenticeship as a sound engineer with the BBC at their Manchester studios. He was aware that Geoff had been involved with many BBC programmes, including outside broadcasts for "Workers Playtime" with Wilfred Pickles.

Geoff, who was now an instructor at the University, joined HBA in February 1964 and brought his superior technical broadcasting experience to a team of enthusiastic volunteers, where no such experience existed.

The "recording studio" was immediately taken under his wing and moved away from a Toc H bedroom, to Geoff's garden shed.

Geoff also became interested in the quality of the transmissions to the hospitals and with reception of our programmes at the patients' bedside.

His first technical task was to improve the Chest Hospital broadcasts by building a new amplifier using transistors, to replace the old Rediffusion valve amplifier, in order to boost the output around the wards.

He also quickly arranged for the GPO to change their private lines from "speech lines" to "music lines" to cater for the music now being played.

The music section committee was desperately seeking to establish their own studio and the cellar at Toc H was under serious consideration.

However in July 1964, Geoff, with his extensive knowledge of broadcasting, prepared a four page closely-typed technical report for the committee to consider.

He posed the question: "Is the Cellar to be a recording studio or a radio transmitting studio?" So far a radio transmission studio had not been seriously considered.

This was such a major change in the history of HBA that it is necessary to "go back to the beginning" to understand the point of Geoff's very dramatic report.

From 1952 to 1964 the football commentary GPO line and the pre-recorded music request tapes were fed into the Rediffusion operating base at Lyon Street, next door to the Royal South Hants Hospital.

The Rediffusion network, a private landline copper wire system, was wired around central Southampton and out to the Southampton Hospitals and they were, at that time, broadcasting 3 radio programmes: Home and Light on channels A and B and a "foreign" programme on channel C.

The foreign programme was selected by the Rediffusion engineers from either "Athlone" an Irish music channel, or "Hilversum" a Dutch radio station and in the evenings it was usually "Radio Luxembourg".

The Rediffusion system also, later on, transmitted on other channels a high quality sound only output for the BBC and ITV television programmes. This was for the benefit of their residential customers who rented a TV monitor, and not relevant to the Hospital broadcasts. The hospital wall switches only had three active channels to choose from.

In order to broadcast the HBA Football commentary and our music tapes, a Rediffusion engineer would have to visit each hospital to switch on the local hospital amplifier. This Rediffusion amplifier, receiving the HBA transmission via a copper wire from the Rediffusion base, would then broadcast the HBA programme over channel C on the radio dials in the hospital wards.

The only exception to this system, was the transmission to the Fred Woolley Home of Recovery. They were not on the Rediffusion private copper wire circuit, but received their Rediffusion programmes broadcast via an FM frequency, broadcast to the two FM tuners located at Fred Woolley House.

(They were later connected to HBA on a GPO spur line, from our Winchester Road location, which was very close by)

Geoff's major proposal was to take over the Rediffusion Channel C on a permanent basis and bypass the Rediffusion Lyon Street facility by the use of an HBA-controlled GPO line network. This would eliminate the need to send an engineer out every time we wished to broadcast.

However, we would only use their channel C when we were actually broadcasting; the rest of the time it would transmit the regular Rediffusion output.

This would initially require the existing GPO line running from the Dell to Rediffusion to be re-routed to run from the Dell out to the Toc H Building at Winchester Road, Bassett.

The new outgoing GPO line circuit, controlled by HBA would now be run from the Toc H broadcasting studio to all the Southampton Hospitals.

If the committee decided that the cellar would only be required as a sound recording studio then his comments regarding the transmission of radio programmes would not be relevant. However if the committee wished to use the cellar for broadcasting purposes three significant items needed consideration:-

Firstly, funds would have to be found to pay for the rental and installation of the HBA-controlled GPO line network and the moving of the football line.

Secondly, every amplifier in all the hospitals would have to be upgraded to a transistorised system (prototype already built by Geoff).

Thirdly, the amplifiers at Rediffusion would require the installation of a remote transistorised switching mechanism, which could be actioned from the HBA studio at the start of their transmission. At the end of the HBA programme they could then automatically be switched back to the Rediffusion transmissions once again. Geoff had already built a similar working prototype, which he had installed in the amplifier at the Chapel in the RSH, to meet the Vicar's requirements, and it became known as the Vicar's Switch.

At the music committee meeting on 6th August 1964 the Treasurer reported the bank balance stood at £171, but Geoff's GPO line system was estimated to need almost £300. (This was in addition to the £300 estimate already on the agenda for the cellar studio building works).

It was resolved:

(a) the Toc H cellar studio would be constructed initially only for tape-recording purposes and also to be used as a record library.

(b) no alteration to the existing GPO line contracts at present.

(c) when funds became available, the cellar would be turned into a transmission studio with all the GPO lines being connected thereto.

As the committee had already established that it would cost around £300 to refurbish the cellar, this was given priority over the technical introduction of our own GPO line network.

At the October 1964 meeting Geoff was promoted to the post of Chief Engineer, probably not only because of his technical skills, but also in recognition of all the many hours of backbreaking and dirty work he and his team of engineering assistants had endured in clearing out the cellars, and helping to prepare them as a recording studio.

However, in the meantime, Geoff had put his thinking cap on and decided that, if they rented a GPO line at a cost of £2.00 per annum, connecting the cellar studio to the GPO Bassett Exchange, they would be able to "go live" on the GPO line circuitry at very little expense. This £2.00 was agreed to be paid for out of the Football section funds and now Geoff was relieved of his building renovation duties and asked to concentrate on his studio radio transmission project.

Rediffusion had by now donated all their old valve-driven hospital amplifiers to HBA and Geoff and his team had upgraded each of them with the transistorised amplification adjustments, so two out of his three technical innovations had been completed.

All that remained was to take over the line system with a private GPO network under the control of HBA. This could only take place when the studio was ready for transmission.

A Committee meeting in 1969 held in the Toc H Dining Room above the Cellar studio.

Clockwise round the table from extreme left: Alan Lambourn, Guy Garrett, Daphne Rood, Marjorie Sullivan, Frank Fielder, Ken Flood, Geoff Allcock, Leslie Sullivan, John Stranger, Maureen Stranger, Alexandra Bejda, Peter Simpkin and Roger Higgins.

This was a time-consuming and very technical process, as all the equipment had to be hand-built. The volunteer engineers, working under Geoff's guidance in their spare time, were very successful. Geoff's GPO line circuit was now following many different traces around Southampton, however all of them were bouncing back along the single wire from the studio to the Bassett Exchange so in September 1965, a second GPO line was connected to our studio, to alleviate the overload.

On 2nd January 1966 the first live programme was transmitted from the Cellar Studio and HBA was now "in business" as a radio station.

Such were the technical innovations that Geoff had introduced at HBA that, over the course of his further studies at Southampton University he obtained his M.Phil degree in 1968, using as his thesis the work he had implemented at HBA. Really ground-breaking technology.

CHAPTER 4

The Garden Shed

1964 to 1966

Geoff Allcock, as well as being a trained BBC engineer was also a radio ham and had his radio equipment set up in his garden shed. This shed was about the size of a garage and when Geoff heard the quality of the tapes we were broadcasting he quickly took command of their production.

Geoff had three young children indoors so his radio equipment, lovingly hand built, was kept away from the house in the shed he had purchased especially for his hobby. The shed (or shack) was a regular wooden structure, but he had lined the walls and ceiling with soundproofing materials and also as a protection from the weather - he spent hours and hours at his hobby - he always had a piece of equipment under construction.

Each Tuesday evening Geoff invited to his shed Ralph Mason, Barry West and John Gibbons, young bright and enthusiastic engineers and, using a valve-driven mixer, two Garrard Turntables and a Brenell Tape-recorder they recorded the request programmes. Truvox tape machines were also used and the slipping mat technique was used on the gram units, all made up by Geoff.

The record request postcards were organised and introduced initially by John Stranger. Geoff then persuaded Penny Gill, one of his University colleagues, to help John with the talking. Later Zena Millard joined the team, and between them they produced two one-hour programmes each Tuesday evening.

Ralph Mason, who worked as an engineer at Rediffusion, carried the completed tapes down to their operations room the next day. His neighbour an electrician called Barry West who worked at HBA with him was about the same age as Ralph and he stayed at HBA only for a few years. By coincidence another member also called Barry West joined HBA around 1974. These two young men are about 8 years apart in their ages, but this has caused many debates amongst the old hands who are still around today who confuse these two in their memories.

The quality of the tape-recordings improved dramatically, even though they were produced in a garden shed that was sometimes so fuggy with cigarette smoke that by the end of each evening a Health and Safety officer would today condemn the workplace. John, Penny and Zena did not smoke, but the engineers, who were not allowed to speak, or make a noise whilst recording, found relaxation in quietly smoking up a storm. One of Geoff's regular comments was "What's that funny smell?" It was, in fact, the smell of fresh air when the shed door was opened.

Tension sometimes filled the air, as well as smoke, and if the machinery was not functioning correctly it was not unusual to see Geoff rip off his headphones and throw them across the room. He never lost his temper with the people, only with the equipment. The surprise feature of this act however was that they always seemed to fly out of the open window on to the lawn (his respect for the equipment was always greater than his rage, and it only happened in the summer when the window was open.)

Another enthusiastic radio ham, who joined the team at that time was Paul Shoosmith. Paul started his career at HBA by helping the engineers build and operate the equipment in the shed and he remained as an active member for about 25 years. Paul was the outside broadcast engineer in charge of the musical broadcasts from the Dance Halls in the late 60's and early 70's, bringing wonderful big band sounds to the listeners live from The Pier, Top Rank Suite and the Guildhall.

When Geoff was not in his shed he was often found to be working in his own time at the University, building kit for HBA, and sometimes the evening crew would carry on without him.

On one occasion a film crew from Southern Television spent the whole day in the shed making a feature for "Three Go Round" showing how young people were putting something back into society. Geoff, of course, was at work so he left John Gibbons in charge of his precious shed.

Geoff left strict instructions and said that whatever happens they should not film the Aerial tower outside the shed as he did not want to give the impression that the HBA programmes were transmitted by radio.

Of course the opening shot in the television piece was a long tracking shot down the tower to the shed. Geoff was not happy! Also the portable lights that were used inside the shed nearly set light to the roof and the ceiling was severely burnt. Had John been an employee he would have been sacked, but Geoff later forgave him.

Ralph Mason had been introduced to Geoff's engineering team by Ken Flood, his supervisor in his day job. Ralph also attended the local technical college with John Gibbons and when it was suggested to John that there was a man working in his shed looking for help to build equipment for a radio station John needed little persuasion to join.

John not only joined the engineering crew but he also became a great ambassador for HBA, he introduced Zena Millard and Guy Garrett to the team and when Penny Gill left he was asked to find a replacement for her.

He travelled everywhere with Ralph Mason, recording many interesting interviews for the HBA programmes and at one stage he knocked on the front door of a potential replacement for Penny. When the young lady opened the door, her very young brother threw himself into John's arms shouting "Daddy". Ralph, who was with him, failed to operate his portable tape recorder at that moment, but the smirk on Ralph's face took weeks to wear off.

Life in the shed was a bit of a crush, the mixer operator was seated, the gram deck operator stood and the presenter would be seated behind them. Geoff would perch on the bench in the corner with his hand hovering over the tape unit and everyone else would stand, crouch or sit on the floor. The multi-coloured carpet is still there today, so it was obviously fairly substantial to cope with the hordes of visitors.

It really was a tight squeeze at times and once, just after John Gibbons had started there, in an effort to move back, put his elbow through the glass pane on the shed door. Geoff's only concern was to pick up the pieces and carry on recording. John brought a new piece of glass the next day and nothing more was ever said about it.

Perhaps the star of this era of HBA was Mary Allcock, who allowed the hordes of weird people to invade her garden every Tuesday evening and later allowed Geoff to devote so much of his spare time to HBA's historical beginnings.

CHAPTER 5

The Cellar Studio

1966 to 1969

The studio equipment in the early years was all designed and built by Geoff, and he "resigned" many times due to his equipment regularly being flooded out at the Toc H basement studio (more of that later).

By April 1964, just one year after the first meeting of the newly-formed music section of HBA, programmes were extended to two evenings per week. In addition to the Saturday football commentaries and the Wednesday evening request programme another evening request programme on Fridays was added.

The third evening music programme was started in June 1964 with the installation of the GPO line to the Children's Hospital in Winchester Road with a special request programme for children, broadcast on Saturday evenings, from 6.30pm to 7.15pm.

All broadcasts at this stage continued to be transmitted from the pre-recorded tapes played from the Rediffusion network offices in Lyon Street.

There were never sufficient funds to meet the financial demands of the growing organisation and annual subscriptions were increased in 1965 from half a crown up to five shillings per annum. Although the equipment was hand-built and records were still being donated and borrowed, GPO line rentals and tapes and request cards still had to be paid for. At one point it was minuted that 4 records on loan from P A Baker had been damaged so HBA had to buy them! However, records were seldom purchased.

With the enthusiasm of Geoff and his engineering crew, expansion of the service to new locations was always a priority and additional GPO lines were connected to Hillfield Home for the Blind and also to the Old Folks' Home at Brownhill.

Throughout 1964 and 1965 the volunteers met in various rooms at the Toc H premises at the top of the Avenue (usually the kitchen or dining room). It was a great day, well-documented, when the very first music programme was transmitted live from the new studio, constructed in the basement. This went out live on Sunday 2nd January 1966.

Here, two years after the start of the music section, is where HBA joined the swinging 60's with their very own live radio music station, dramatically extending the radio service, which began 14 years earlier with the football commentaries.

Another milestone recorded in the minutes of HBA - Alan Lambourn was appointed to the position of Studio Manager on 1st March 1966, just after the studio went live, having been an active member since June 1964. Today 38 years later he still holds the same position but he is now called the Studio Director.

It was the swinging sixties throughout the UK, and at Southampton Hospital Radio the music and entertainment programmes were also swinging with many pioneering moves being made in the engineering department.

Greater coverage and more listeners continued to be the aim of the executive committee and, by 1969, the service was now being broadcast to ten locations :- The General, Royal South Hants, Chest, Eye, Fred Woolley House, Winchester Hospital, the Children's Hospital, the Children's Annexe at Bursledon, Hillfield Home for the Blind and Brownhill House Old People's Home. It was reported in the minutes that our service was now available to over 1600 listeners.

GPO lines were also being installed to bring in live outside broadcasts, not only from the football and cricket grounds, but also lines coming in from the Gaumont Theatre (now called the Mayflower), the Southampton Guildhall, The Top Rank Suite and The Mecca Ballroom on the Pier. The latter two venues were very much a part of the local swinging sixties, but both have now been overtaken by housing developments.

In 1969 a delegation of John Stranger, Geoff Allcock and Lesley Sullivan went to the Houses of Parliament to lobby their MP for Hospital Radio stations to be granted a special radio licence to broadcast on the airwaves. This was not a success and the MP's said that we were ahead of our time.

The minutes in 1969 showed there were 60 paid-up members plus a few members who had not paid their subs, but by the middle of the 70's the numbers had risen to almost 90 active members. From the mid 80's onwards there have always been around 100 people on our books.

All were volunteers and right from the start of HBA, and even 50 years on, it has been the principle that no-one received any remuneration or expenses for their services.

Programmes were therefore only possible during "out of work hours" in the evenings, and the weekend programme schedules started at lunchtime on Saturdays.

The "Hospital Radio Times" booklets were now being professionally printed and distributed around the wards each month. The advertisers, whose name appeared in them, funded these monthly booklets, and the next chapter is a copy of our programmes for the first week of November 1969.

There were occasional blips in the transmission for example, the following item has been reproduced from the minutes of the April 1968 meeting:-

"Following a complaint from the residents of Hillfield Home for the Blind, that they were not receiving our transmissions, it was discovered that the loudspeaker had been removed, and then returned, but not reconnected, by an unauthorised person stating he was from HBA. After enquiries, it was found that this person was mentally ill. No further action taken"

In 1969 the Requestline telephone number was 67675 and there were over 2000 logged calls for musical requests.

With the great expansion of our network by 1970 our GPO annual line rental and call charges exceeded £4,000 and this was to be a serious problem in the years ahead.

The entrance into the cellar.

Our first home with dirt floors and plant life everywhere (inside and out)

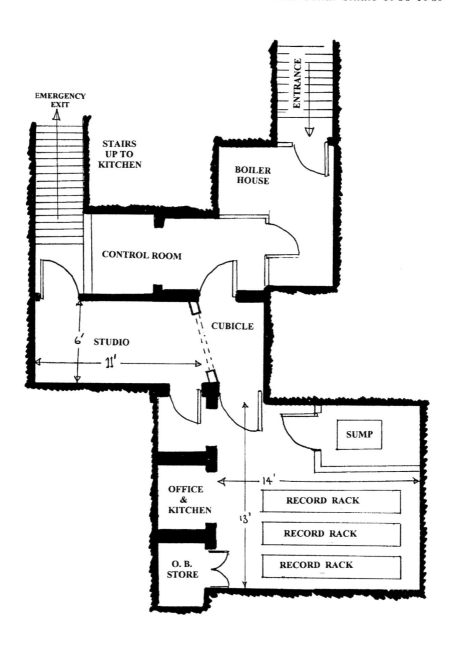

Plan of the Toc H Cellar Studio

CHAPTER 6

Programmes Schedule
November 1969

The "Hospital Broadcasting Times" Programmes for the first week in November 1969 (noting that all times are pm)

Saturday 1st November

1.00   FOR THE CHILDREN
Children's own requests presented by Barbara Bond, and a "Quipple" story from Valery

2.40   MUSICAL INTERLUDE

2.50   ASSOCIATION FOOTBALL
Commentary on the 1st Division Match, Saints v. West ham.

4.45   SPORTS NEWS (BBC)

6.00   THE NATIONAL NEWS

6.05   IN TUNE TONIGHT
Your Saturday evening entertainment from HBA consists of music old and new, your requests, the latest news, two trips downtown with Paul to the Mecca Ballroom for dance music from the Eddie King Set.

Sunday 2nd November

7.00   MUSIC TO REMEMBER
A varied selection of music presented by Jim Barnes

7.20   SUNDAY REQUESTS
The guest D.J. tonight is Dennis Skillicorn

7.40   AMONG OUR 78's
Some more tunes from the "dinner plate" discs in our library presented by Guy Garrett

8.10   THEN SINGS MY SOUL
The words and music for Sunday

8.40   MUSICAL INTERLUDE

9.00   MORE REQUESTS
By card and phone just for you

9.50   EPILOGUE
Produced by Ian Ward

Monday 3rd November

7.30   THE ALAN ROSS SHOW
Some requests and melodies from The Alan Ross Sound '69. It's introduced by Paul Shoosmith from the Top Rank Suite.

8.00   EVENING SERENADE
The World's greatest songs and tunes from a different composer each week, introduced by Philip Farlowe.

8.15   MY FAVOURITE THINGS
Your chance to star on the
programme when Pam, Eric and
Chris call in at the Royal South
Hants Hospital.

9.15   FROM SUE TO YOU
Requests by card and phone
presented by Sue Polyblank

Pritchett Brown in which he
introduces some humorous extracts.
Peter hopes these will cause a grin,
a chuckle or a hearty laugh.

9.15   TURNTABLE
Dennis Dexter is keeping the table
turning this evening with your
REQUESTS

Tuesday 4th November

8.00   JAKE'S PLACE
Your monthly visit to the home of
Clive Jacobs, accompanied by Mrs
Chips for your REQUESTS

8.30   H. B. A. GUEST
A chat with a well known person
and their choice of music

9.00   RETURN TO JAKE'S
PLACE
For more Requests and news of
events happening this month in
Southampton from Clive.

Thursday 6th November

8.00   LISTEN WITH MARY
To your REQUESTS

8.30   MUSIC   HALL
MEMORIES
Music that entertained audiences
from the stage stars of this century.
Our master of Ceremonies - Peter
Pritchett Brown

9.00   MORE FROM MARY
Why not ring Mary for a chat and
hear your favourite record -
Southampton 67675

Wednesday 5th November

7.00   CHILDREN'S REQUESTS
From Southampton and Winchester.
Collected by "Uncle Eddie".
Presented by Barbara

8.25   REMEMBER THIS ONE
That's the question Allan St. John
Holt asks his guests as he delves
among the older pop records stored
in our library.

9.00   MAKE 'EM LAUGH
The first of a new series from Peter

Friday 7th November

8.00   REQUESTS FROM YOUR
MAN FRIDAY
John Stranger

8.30   SPORTS LINE UP
A complete guide to local and
national sport from Lloyd
Woodland, John Stranger and Ken
Fielder.

8.55   MORE MAN FRIDAY
Means more requests from John

CHAPTER 7

Moving Out

1969 to 1970

BROADCASTING FROM THE BASEMENT AT Toc H

"IS NOT MUCH FUN"

An extract from the minutes of a November 1966 meeting woefully states that " Once again water has come through the ceiling of the studio. This was the fifth time in as many weeks"

A new and improved studio facility would be every member's dream but funds for such a dream were beyond the realms of possibility, except, that is, to Arthur Leslie Sullivan, the founder of Southampton Hospital Radio with his football commentaries, and now holding the position as the Appeals Organiser and Chief Fund-raiser.

He was also well aware, as a committee member, of the trials and tribulations that broadcasting from a basement had brought them.

Premises in Anglesea Road, Shirley were offered, but they were on the second floor and dramatic calculations about how the floors would need to be strengthened to take the weight of the record library (mostly donated 78's) put an end to that plan.

From the committee minutes in December 1966 the following was recorded: "The Chairman is to write a letter of thanks to the Hospital Management Committee stating that a plot of land at the Chest Hospital would be quite satisfactory for a new studio".

Whilst this was the seed of an idea in the back of Leslie's mind, in 1966 such a move was too much of a leap into the dark. It was also of great concern that the Chest Hospital site at that time was likely to be sold, as it was not included in the Hospital Authorities long term plans.

He did however lead the drive to raise the funds for the first purpose-built studio for Southampton Hospital Radio to be constructed in the grounds of the Winchester Road, Toc H property. This location was also known to be only available in the short term and a brick building was not considered to be a good investment. A lease was never signed on this site, we stayed there purely on a "gentleman's agreement".

The following details have been reproduced from a 1969 Hospital Broadcasting Association booklet :-

BELIEVE IT OR NOT . . . .

..... programmes come from an excavated cellar and despite an automatic pump to keep down the water level, our carpets on occasions are more like Chinese paddy fields !

..... conditions are so cramped that everybody constantly breathes in to allow others to pass to and from the control cubicle, record library or studio. Grand names for what are little more than dug-outs !

..... composite programmes cannot be recorded or new members receive technical training until the evening transmission closes down at 10pm. Not the best time to commence a few hours work !

..... prospective members can be excused if their initial impression is that our only qualification is expert sardine packers ! Whereas in reality they are most welcome and much needed. As for essential sub-section meetings, we surely must be the most modern of the wandering tribes !

..... expensive equipment, largely created by the skill and devotion of our chief engineer and his henchmen, simply cannot be given the proper stowage and care it so richly deserves - indeed somehow must receive, if we are to remain financially solvent.

..... our typewriter queues up with the tea pot to use the one small table possible, in an ill-spared corner of the record library !

..... we are doing our best under near impossible conditions, which almost verge on being unhygienic !

WE WOULD BE DELIGHTED any evening if you care to see the set up for yourselves. Go up the drive of Toc H Mark V (off Bassett Roundabout) to the house. Try not to bump into an oil tank when turning left, nor tumble down the steep stone steps to the boiler room. At the bottom, give the boiler a wide berth, but not so as to fall over bundles of newspapers stacked for sale on behalf of the funds, and our door clearly will be seen, provided someone has put on the light ! Admittedly, this sounds more than a little adventurous, but then HBA itself always has been, and ever will, continue to be a high-hearted adventure.

Obviously, these conditions must be improved if at least the present standards are to be maintained; even more if the programmes in terms of scope and quality are to attain the still higher standards which are our declared aim and avowed intention.

By good fortune, Toc H generously has agreed to lease an adjoining plot of land (2,000 sq.ft.) at a nominal rent and planning consent has been obtained to construct the projected new studios, technical facilities, expanded record library and essential supporting facilities.

The cost of our new studios is estimated to be £7,500 and it is hoped that charitably-minded organisations and individuals will come to our aid with suggestions or by themselves arranging additional events in order to meet this target.

This booklet is signed: A.L.Sullivan - Hon. Appeal Organiser.

Due to the incredible fund-raising energies of Leslie, on the 9th February 1970, the prefabricated studio building was erected on the site. It also transpired that, in 1970, Leslie was the President of Southampton Rotary - such perfect timing!

CHAPTER 8

Above Ground

1970 to 1980

With this new decade, another phase in our history was to unfold. In August 1970, the second newsletter issued by John Stranger started on a sad note to record his leaving the team. Having been the guiding light and the chairman since the inception of the "music section" in 1963, John was moving to a new job in Tamworth, Leicester.

Before he left, however, the Association had been formed into a registered charity and brand new, purpose-built studios were being finalised for what was by then a thriving group of over 60 members, producing amazingly sophisticated radio programmes to 10 hospital locations around Southampton.

Geoff and his team designed the new studio complex, based on the idea that all the wiring and the two operating studios would be along one side of the building. Meeting rooms, the Library and all administrative activities would be down the other side, separated by a corridor, in order to keep noise levels in the sound studios to a minimum.

This same basic feature was continued into the third and also into the fourth studio building, even though the third and fourth buildings employed architects to assist in their design.

Geoff's hand built scale model of the studio (see picture) was then used not only for the engineering designs but also by Leslie Sullivan as his prime tool in raising the funds to pay for its construction.

In 1970, the major engineering task was to move from the cellar to the new studios above ground, without going off-air. As live transmissions were being broadcast every day this was a serious problem, but Geoff Allcock and his team managed to achieve this without a hitch.

However in August, just a short while before the opening, a thief broke into the new premises through a fire door and stole the top 30 hit records that had been laid-out for the children's programme. He also stole microphones, amplifiers, speakers from the walls and control units from the desktops. These were not just off-the-shelf units but each item had been lovingly hand-built by our engineers especially for the job in hand and were all incredibly difficult to replace in such a short time.

The publicity was marvellous for HBA and even a quote from a member of the underworld was published in the press as "Robbing charities got crime a bad name".

The thief was caught, but the equipment, which was later recovered from a field in Winchester, was useless, as it had been left out in the rain.

Insurance monies were received to compensate, but Geoff and his team of four technical engineers slaved through many late nights at the laboratories at Southampton University to build the units again.

The thief was ordered to pay damages of £400 at the rate of £5 per week, but the minutes only record that we recovered £25 from him in total. Bonhomie came to our immediate rescue, just as soon as they heard of our plight, with a special cheque for £250. This was in addition to the regular donations they were making towards our running costs.

On 2nd August 1971 the final move from the old Cellar studio to the new above ground building took place. On the final day many nostalgic tears were shed as wires were cut and the cellars stripped. The official opening ceremony by Earl Mountbatten was scheduled for October 12th 1971.

Enthusiasm amongst the members was on a high with hundreds of man (and woman) hours put into the internal construction requirements of the new studio building - as well as on fund-raising activities.

In 1971, Alexandra Bejda produced some wonderful quarterly newsletters, detailing some of the personalities who were around at that time.

Peter Maggs temporarily took over the chairman's role when John Stranger left, but at the AGM in January 1971, Peter Pritchett-Brown was formally elected by the members as the new chairman.

Bryan Dowding as Chief Administrator, Graham Fielder as editor of the HBA Times and Chris Litton as the Waste Paper Collection coordinator had all been members for quite a few years before their 1970 official appointments, and they are still members of HBA more than 30 years later.

Pete Simpkin created the role of "Transmission Controller" - one for each evening; in order to make each day's programme output the responsibility of one person. There were training courses for operators also special training for operators to deal with telephone calls, but no organised training for presenters.

Dr Edwin Course, from Southampton University, was introduced by John Stranger in an attempt to uplift the quality of the presenters.

Chris and Wendy Bowes were put in charge of "Personnel" to cope with the flood of newcomers and the whole Association was taking on a new regime.

Dennis Skillicorn was voted "HBA's most popular DJ" and Phillip Molyneux was the Public Relations Officer, having formerly been Head of Presentation & Programmes.

Allan St. John Holt was heavily involved in the "Waste Paper Department" and John Challis, the manager at HBA's own NatWest Bank, was the official Treasurer. Both of these members were later destined to take over the chairman's role.

As well as producing radio programmes every day, the members were also continuously fund-raising. In July 1970 the Southampton Carnival floats included a Giant Bed-pan, Hospital Bed, and the HBA Outside Broadcast Caravan, all manned by HBA. Whilst our members raised over £50 towards the Carnival collection we actually received more than £1,600 from the total Carnival funds to purchase an electronic console for our new studio.

By the end of the 70's, Hospital Radio was by now achieving national recognition as a positive influence on the care of patients. There was a large new Hospital being built in London and part of the construction plan was for £10,000 to be set aside for the installation of radio equipment and the setting-up of a charity to run the hospital radio station.

With the new facilities new alliances were being forged and the Talking Newspapers for the Blind were given studio space to record their audio tapes.

The Winchester Road Toc H Building in the background, with a concrete base laid out in their garden ready for the erection of our "Above Ground" studio. Here is the first delivery of the prefabricated sections in 1969.

The Studio under construction at Winchester Road.
The Chaplain's House in the background and the Stable Block in the foreground. Both became temporary homes for our expanding Record Library.

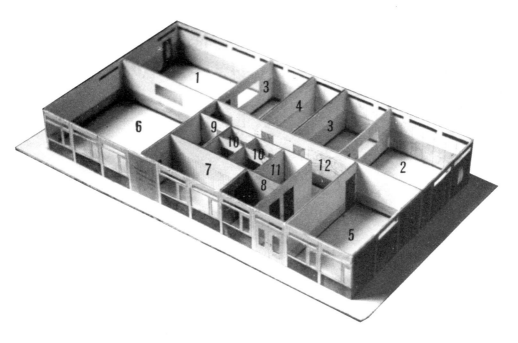

1. STUDIO ONE	7. KITCHEN
2. STUDIO TWO	8. CLOAK ROOM
3. MIXING ROOM	9. OFFICE
4. CONTROL ROOM	10. TOILETS
5. RECORD LIBRARY	11. O. B. EQUIPMENT
6. MEETING ROOM	12. CORRIDOR

Notice the two operational studios - one for "on air" and one for preparing programmes - such luxury.

Geoff Allcock's Model

Our first real studio building constructed in prefabricated panels and a whole world away from the cramped underground cellars.

Ashley Sutton and Graham Fielder inside the Winchester Road Studio in 1975

Earl Mountbatten signing the visitors book in the new Library with Bryan Dowding to his right and Peter Pritchett-Brown on his left. Marjorie Sullivan is looking over his shoulder.

Earl Mountbatten of Burma helping with the opening programme from our new studio in 1971. He was the very first contributor to HBA with a cheque for £10 made as a donation towards the football section funds in 1952.

"Our Gang" in 1971

Left to right Leslie Sullivan, Marie Fielder, Barry West, Graham Fielder, John Challis, Elizabeth Kinloch, Helen Cox, Ashley Sutton, David Doling, Marjorie Sullivan, Bryan Dowding, Clare Rowthorne, Barry Jackson, Ann Tupper, Martyn Tupper and Ken Flood

Alan Lambourn on a Saturday afternoon in 1970, compiling the cricket results, watching the Rugby on TV, operating the equipment and talking - all at the same time. The essential skills of the Saturday Sports controller. (This role was taken over by Tony Harding around 1977 and 25 years later Tony is still the Sports controller.)

John Stranger in a relaxed mood when the studio first opened in 1969. Notice the furniture!

Leslie Arthur Sullivan (Sully) at the microphone, with Geoff Allcock concentrating on his every word and Guy Garrett in the background.

CHAPTER 9

The 3rd Studio
1980 to 1990

Having been evicted from our Bassett site the pioneering enthusiasm of the engineers began to wane. Geoff Allcock, the first Chief Engineer retired from his post in 1973 and was replaced by Clive John. Clive had been actively involved for many years as an engineer when he took control of the reins, not only monitoring the internal engineering equipment and attempting to maintain the fabric of the building, but also controlling the fairly active team of outside broadcast enthusiasts.

Clive was involved in planning the 1980 GPO lines and network changes needed for the move to our third studio, but decided to leave the Association before the huge new wiring installation at our third studio began. Phil Soper, who joined HBA in 1977, assumed the mantle of Chief Engineer in 1979 a post he still holds today, over 25 years later. Pauline his wife, joined as a member in 1986 and recently received her 15 year certificate of merit for duties above and beyond the call. Pauline, now the Head Librarian, often spends more time at HBA than Phil.

Norman Woodford a local architect, helped design the structures of both the second and the third studio building, but it was Phil Soper along with Ivor Worsley a retired qualified sound engineer, who between them designed and constructed the complete third studio equipment and wiring installation. This time, with Ivor's BBC and ITV contacts, and Phil's contacts at ntl, the studios were fitted-out with equipment from "refurbished, part-used and modified corporation rejects." The desks, turntables, switching gear and sound-proofing were all, once again, hand-built, but to a newer and more modern specification than before. Ivor did most of the studio cabling and Phil worked on the apparatus in the control room.

Tony Harding, who joined in 1973, was anxious to bring in his "American Style" jingles and promos. Phil acquired two NAB Cart machines and HBA bought Tony's own NAB Cart machine. These were all installed in the new studios, plus a rack for Tony's huge stock of Cartridges, once again upgrading our programme presentations.

In 1977 Tony had been promoted to the Saturday Sports presenter's role and every Saturday we also transmitted the Children's programmes, so he was able to really be "with it" and produce top of the pops programmes, which may not have always been appreciated by some of the "old fogeys" on the team. (Nothing's changed !) However we have always tried to meet the wide musical tastes of our listeners.

This was also true of the Friday Fun Show that Tony organised. This programme pushed the boundaries of programming content well out in front and required Phil and Ivor to develop and build more and more complex connections in order to meet the endless demands for more facilities.

Phil and his team had originally designed and built three operating desks centred around a control room rack system. Two studios were wired up fairly quickly but Phil became distracted by the demands of the programme presenters who continually wanted more features. Phil was in his element at this stage (just as Geoff had been 20 years earlier) expanding and experimenting with faster and more intricate technological requirements. And just as soon as he had built and commissioned a new piece of kit, there was a demand on his bench for something new. The third studio was therefore not commissioned until a couple of years later.

With the introduction of the public address activities our contact with the public was being extended and this was a double-edged sword in relation to our programme schedules. More was being expected from us as a radio station and when our programmes did not "get through" we were being publicly criticised.

Programmes were on air seven days a week, with evening schedules starting around 6pm and from midday at the weekends. Training for presenters was now regularly available and no one went on air unless they had passed an audition. Whilst we could control our programme output we had very little control of the reception at the patient's bedside and this was a very depressing time for us as the wiring around the wards in the Hospitals was now over 25 years old.

Technology was moving along and Phil was at this time also involved in reorganising the GPO landline network, which had now been taken over by British Telecom.

The studio equipment was now using integrated circuits, a development one stage up from transistors and semiconductors, which in turn had been a technological development from the valve equipment when Geoff joined. However the old valve amplifiers at the hospitals were squeaking a bit, but still performing well.

With inflation roaring away in the late 1970's, by the early 1980's our landline charges had more than doubled. Services and expenses had to be seriously curtailed in order to strike a balance with our annual fund-raising abilities. The costs of running the new studio were escalating, though volunteers were still not paid any expenses or wages.

Ken Holloway and his Public Address team came to the rescue and quite a few of the "older" programme presenters found a new niche as performers and commentators at Fetes, Shows and Carnivals. These public address gigs also gave jobs to engineering newcomers who wanted something to do. Phil and Ivor found their time being consumed in designing and building the mobile studio in the Bedford vehicle.

We now had a fully equipped outside broadcast caravan as well as the new Public Address vehicle to assist the outside broadcast team. With our name written large on the caravan and the PA vehicle we were becoming better known to the public and this obviously helped with our fund-raising events.

The engineering department, by this time, had burst out of its one small room in the 3rd studio building and two Portacabins were acquired "on loan" and kitted out as the engineers' workshops. These were parked on the concrete apron outside our studio building at the Chest Hospital site and this had the added advantage of keeping the studios a bit tidier as well as providing more space for the engineers to work.

Although an eyesore in themselves they did lead to us having a larger new studio building when Tesco came along.

Lord Romsey, the grandson of Earl Mountbatten of Burma, with Lady Romsey performing the opening ceremony of our third studio in December 1981.

Tony Harding in full operating mode, inserting a cartridge into the new Discart Machines in 1981, at the same time as operating the desk and doing the talking as well.

Phil Soper (left) and Ivor Worsley at one of the three control desks in November 1980, checking their wiring schemes and monitoring the systems they had designed and installed prior to handing over the studios to the presenters and operators. Constructing and installing their handcrafted equipment took up a huge amount of their time, with Phil taking time off work to complete the many tasks. Fortunately Ivor had just retired from his day job and spent two or three months full-time on the wiring installations.
(Photograph courtesy of Southampton Daily Echo)

Ivor in the Apparatus Room (Control Room) in 1980. Connections were made by using GPO jack plugs.

18th October 1982 was the 30th Anniversary of Southampton Hospital Radio and the City Mayor, Mrs Barbara Barfoot, donned headphones to wish Southampton and Winchester HBA a happy 30th Birthday. Guests in the studio included Saints manager Chris Nicholl and his assistant manager John Mortimer. Also present at that event was Leslie Sullivan (75) who had retired from his broadcasting role three years earlier.
(Photograph courtesy of Southampton Daily Echo)

CHAPTER 10
Tesco Money
1990 to 1993

The Chest Hospital site was not included in the long term plans for the Hospital Authorities and in 1986, Tesco started negotiations to purchase one half of the 20 acre site.

Local residents did not want a Tesco Superstore near their home and the local council, who wanted a housing development, refused planning permission. These negotiations took over five years and, in 1991, Tesco, appealed successfully for the construction of a new NHS Administration Office on the site, but their application for a new store was refused.

A four day public enquiry followed in March 1992 at the Civic Centre Council Chambers, with Barristers acting for both parties. I was delighted by the comment made to me by the Tesco Director. He quite confidently gave me permission for all the HBA members to park in the new Tesco car park - this was on the first day of the hearing.

I was intrigued by such a promise, and having sat through the hearing and marvelled at the efficiency of the organisation behind Tesco, I became a Tesco fan. Previously I had only really known them as a shop selling groceries.

The formal documentation in support of the Tesco appeal was a pile of books about 18 inches high. The council's response documents were less than 2 inches high. The sheer volume of information and depth of their arguments in support of the appeal totally overwhelmed the investigator and his judgement was not surprisingly in their favour. Approval for the new store was granted in June 1992.

At that time construction of new out of town stores was in vogue and from a review of the Tesco accounts it was not surprising to note they opened 24 new stores in 1992 and 26 in 1993.

Having seen their administration and organisation in action it was quite evident that nothing was left to chance, and when they approached me to knock down our studio building, I was well aware of the organisation behind their request.

The original scheme for the 20 acre Chest Hospital site was for a dividing line running east to west. Ten acres would remain in the Health Authority's control and a new "Western Hospital" was to be constructed on the northern half of the site from the proceeds of the sale. Tesco would acquire the southern half of the site and they would contract to build a new NHS Trust Administration building in one corner of their site.

Eventually the new Western Hospital was actually built in 1996 from the sale proceeds of this deal.

The parcel of land occupied by Hospital Radio sat neatly on the north/south dividing line, with the planned new hospital on one side of us and the new Tesco Store on the other. Thus HBA members would have the benefit of the Tesco car park on one side of our building and enjoy the secluded grounds of the new hospital on the other.

However that was only plan A. Plan B was much better. Around the perimeter of the "new hospital site", but land-locked, the local council owned an L shaped parcel of land situated alongside Tebourba Way on one side and running along the rear of the houses on Redbridge Hill on the other. The council really wanted access to this site, as there was room for them to build 70 houses.

Tesco were unhappy with the Plan A entrance to their Store, scheduled to be from Oakley Road. This required the road to be widened and not really the best access for the stream of lorries and cars expected.

Access for their store and petrol filling station from the Tebourba Way dual carriageway would be ideal, so Tesco re-opened negotiations with the Council with a view to giving them access to their land-locked site.

If Tesco could have their entrance direct from Tebourba Way, they would provide, free of charge, a road into the council owned property.

New Traffic Lights would be required to break into the dual carriageway, but lights already existed at Oakley Road and at the Winchester Road junction and these were considered to be quite close together. The highway authorities did agree to allow a new set of lights - provided they were near the centre of the two existing junctions.

This was the first piece of good news for us - our studio was situated exactly in the location Tesco were instructed to build their new entrance-way. We had to move !

The second piece of good fortune - we had a 21 year lease issued by the Health Authority on the parcel of land our studio was occupying, with 13 years still to run. So Tesco said - "No problem, we will be saving £130,000 on the road-widening project in Oakley Road that we no longer require, so you can have that sum to go away"

Their architect said it would cost £118,000 to replace our existing building so there would be a balance of £12,000 for new equipment

Within a few weeks, rough quotations were obtained for the equipment we would need which alone was likely to cost £75,000.

Thanks for the offer, but no thanks, like Oliver, we wanted more !

In the meantime, the Tesco planning department had prepared their construction timetable for their store, and petrol filling station and they published a planned opening date for November 1994

As mentioned earlier, they opened 26 stores in 1993 - this was 1991 - so their store opening programme was not going to be upset by little old Southampton Hospital Radio.

The first movement in their new store chess game, was to open the Tebourba Way access point. As our studio was in the way, it became the first object which had to be moved.

They appointed their architect to talk to us, instructed him to move us out of the way and ignored the price tag. Our request was simple - a new building please - just one hundred yards up the road on a new piece of leased land.

The architect drew up his sketches on the assumption he would provide a new building similar to the one we already had. But what about the loss of our engineers Portacabins? Words from head office "you cannot have Portacabins alongside our new store, we will make your new building one metre wider and one metre longer to allow you to incorporate your engineers workshops".

Thank you - what about the extensive equipment and wiring installations in the new building ?

"You have three studios at present you can move them one by one into the new building".

A quick discussion with our chief engineer established that although we did have three studios they had been built one on top of each other from an engineering point of view and they could not be dis-assembled individually. It would also not be possible for our engineers to build the new systems in the timescale under review.

This is when our third major influential angel flew in the window. The hospital authorities stated that the project could only proceed as long as Hospital Radio did not go off the air.

This meant that we had to keep the existing broadcasting facilities working whilst constructing the new ones. We would have to have new operating desks and in order to meet the Tesco construction timetable the desks and wiring installations would have to be done by professional contractors. Three quotations were obtained and we "accepted" after some fine tuning, the sum of £82,000. This was for three operating desks and underfloor wiring connected to five sound studios from a central control room.

Tesco planning department was not interested in such trifling costs - we were in the way of their new store opening - agreed - they wrote the cheque and we placed the order.

At home my bungalow had only a limited ground floor area, so in 1984 I renegotiated my mortgage, had the 22 degree low pitch roof taken off and replaced with a 45 degree roof structure. This was all done to my personal plans, with help from a structural engineer of course, but this doubled the habitable floor area in my little abode.

Why not repeat the exercise for the new HBA studio !

So when the architect said you can have your building one metre longer and one metre wider I also requested a 45 degree roof structure - hence the upper floor space that we have found so useful. Fully carpeted, of course, for sound deadening.

The executive meetings for 18 months were all taken up with the many and varied plans, proposals, ideas and all the requests that we could possibly think of. The engineering department designed and planned the wiring and desks and instructed the contractors accordingly, but the executive collectively planned all the rest of the fittings. Even the lightbox sign and the name thereon was a collective decision, as well as the colour of the tiles on the kitchen floor - not easy when the 10 executive members all expressed their own point of view.

The engineers however, being embarrassed with such a wish list of having their own new studio equipment being manufactured for them, decided to each produce their own "piece of kit". Phil Soper designed and built the Studio Auto Switching Unit, Adrian Wint built the Telephone Switching Unit and Ivor Worsley designed and built the studio clocks.

Phil, Adrian and Ivor specified the desk layouts and the wiring schemes and Mel Bowden from MBI International supplied and installed three MBI Series 20 consoles, along with Sonifex Discarts and a range of other equipment all housed in top purpose-built wooden units.

During the construction phase the Building Contractors, Kyle Stewart, were so impressed with the helpful attitude of HBA they offered us a bonus. We specified the new library shelving, built and stained to our own design, plus the library carousel desk unit. These were all installed without charge and all we paid for was the brand new card index cabinets. The cards were brought over from the old studio. Our new library looked magnificent.

The contract negotiations specified we would supply and install any piece of equipment we could physically carry across from the old studio to the new; eg turntables, carts, etc. However instead of carrying across our "old gear" we took the opportunity to upgrade and bought new. We had invested about £4,000 of our funds in this move.

It cost Tesco almost £400,000, a bit more than their first offer of £130,000.

And Southampton Council in conjunction with a Local Housing Association, built 70 new homes alongside our new studio using the same private access road that we now enjoy.

This development has unfortunately brought with it homes for young vandals and delinquents who have to walk past our magnificent studio building each day. Broken windows and assaults on member's cars have become commonplace and we can no longer leave any HBA vehicles parked outside the studio building.

This our fourth studio is on a new 21 year lease (still at a peppercorn rent of £1.00 per annum) from the Health Authority, commencing from 13th December 1993. The actual land transactions to move us, involved seven different land "swaps" between Tesco, the Council and HBA. The associated legal costs alone would have been beyond our pocket.

We started broadcasting from our new studios on 12th December 1993 and our old building was demolished on 30th December 1993. Tesco opened their superstore in October 1994 - just in time for the Christmas trade - one month earlier than they had planned.

What that did for us though was not only elevate our broadcasting aspirations it also, once again, doubled our studio running costs from £8,000 per annum up to £16,000 per annum. Fund-raising now became even more serious !

Roy Stubbs and Tony Harding in 1992 are studying the plans for the new "Tesco" studio outside the 3rd studio, which is scheduled for demolition.
Note the two OB Caravans in use at that time.
Also note the 22-degree low pitch roof on the old building.

Our 3rd studio built of brick to last forever, but located exactly in the middle of the road where we now drive into the Tesco store.

Our wonderful new studio with the 45 degree pitched roof. Note the inlets in the gable end wall for the air conditioning unit. Unfortunately, the porch glass panels have been smashed so many times by vandals that we have not replaced them.

Roy Stubbs, MC for the day, with Danny LaRue cutting with real scissors and Gordon Sylvester (Tesco Director) assisting him with decorative scissors (coloured in our own shade of blue). In the background is Councillor John Martin the Mayor of Southampton.

I love these traffic lights!
One of the three major reasons why Tesco had to build us a new studio. The
location of the traffic lights was a Highways Authority decision (lucky for us).
(Photograph courtesy of Southampton Daily Echo)

Danny LaRue with his pet dog, Jonti, a Chinese crested hairless, accepts our thank you card - signed by the members - for opening our studio on 12th December 1993.

At the opening ceremony Alan Lambourn holding up a lip microphone similar to the one borrowed by Leslie Sullivan in 1952, in his right hand a set of "war-time cans" which were standard issue in the cellar studio. Emphasising that it was not just a new building we were opening, but also a whole new electronic era, beginning with the equipment we were about to switch on.

Geoff Allcock (left) and John Stranger, meeting again at the opening of our 4th studio in 1993. They first met 30 years earlier and created the "Music Section" between them.

The Executive Committee in December 1993
The opening day ceremony - toasting our thanks to Tesco!
Left to right: Yvonne Lowe, Alan Lambourn, Jennifer Wint, Graham Fielder, Paul Duell,
Sheila Clark, Roy Stubbs, Phil Soper, Ken Holloway and Steve Mullane.
(Photograph courtesy of Southampton Daily Echo)

CHAPTER 11

"Patientline"

1996 to 2002

Just after we had introduced our 24-hour computerised radio service possibly the most significant feature of Southampton Hospital Radio, since its creation 45 years earlier, came about. Our listeners, the patients at the Hospitals, were to be supplied with a personal "Patientline" unit.

Patientline is a commercial firm, independent of the Hospital Authority, who have installed alongside every bed, a unit containing a Television screen, a personal telephone and six radio channels. The patient pays for the use of the TV and telephone by the use of prepaid cards, but the radio service is provided free of charge.

For the first time in 45 years, we became confident that our programmes were now "getting through".

Patientline, a private company, installed their first hospital bedside system in Northwick Park Hospital, Harrow in 1996. Following a couple of visits to Harrow it became quite clear that their system, installed in Southampton, would be a giant leap forward for our service.

Meetings in 1996 and 1997 with the Southampton Hospital Management Committees, where we fully supported the Patientline proposals, culminated in the General, Princess Anne and The Eye Hospitals installing the system in 1998.

The Hospital Radio service at Northwick Park operating only for a few hours each evening was not as sophisticated as the Southampton service. Due to our positive demands for us to have a radio link on their Southampton installation, Hospital Radio became a standard feature on all the Patientline networks across the country. The company has now gone public and raised millions of pounds, for each hospital installation represents a £3million investment, and there are now 36 Hospitals in the UK, and dozens overseas, using the Patientline equipment.

We are confident that our programmes are now reaching the patients 24 hours a day, and, with the aid of the Patientline computerised records, we are also able to determine how many listeners tune in.

It is quite pleasing to record that we are the third most popular station of the six channels available. First choice with around 25% of the listeners is Power FM, a local commercial music station; second choice is BBC Radio Solent. Radio 2 and Hospital Radio are equal third choice with about 15% of the listeners tuned in, followed by the specialist programmes of Radio 4 and Classic FM.

The other interesting feature is to note at what times of the day our audience listens to the radio. Commercial radio stations have their "drive time" in the mornings and at teatimes - these periods are not important to our listeners, but later in the evenings, when the visitors have gone and we play our requests, this now becomes the HBA "prime time"

The Royal South Hants, currently being reorganised and essentially operating as an outpatients unit, still use the old fashioned hard wire FM distribution system around the few wards where they do have overnight patients.

Patientline are currently in negotiation with the Southampton Hospital Authorities to upgrade their units, as this is the fifth year they have been operating. More sophisticated interactive bedside equipment is now available and patients' own hospital records can be stored and accessed alongside their bed. This will make the future bedside unit much more than simply a patient leisure service facility.

CHAPTER 12
Fun and Romance
1963 to 2002

It is not possible to skip through the historical records of our radio station without falling over the fact that hospital radio is both a "people" and "technical" thing. The technical aspects have been well covered down the years, but the Association would be nothing without the many shapes, sizes and personalities of the boys and girls who have made it all happen.

The word romance is such a lovely word and the wedding photograph of Jane and Mike Smith has been selected to highlight this scene. Jane (nee Baron) joined in 1972 and Mike in 1975. They were married in 1977 - a true hospital radio romance.

When you put a group of people together in a "fun situation" it brings out the best in everyone. The trials and tribulations of work, family and home are all left behind when you arrive at the studio or at the outside broadcast gig.

Knowing that what you are doing is in a very small way helping someone else, is also a great aphrodisiac.

There are dozens of happy couples who have (and still do) work together at their hobby of hospital radio. The sorrowful problem is that this happy feeling sometimes makes some couples discontent and they look to the next field for a new relationship.

It therefore follows that we also have a few separations and divorced couples, sometimes due to a hospital radio meeting and sometimes a brand new relationship is formed with another member of the group.

To therefore talk about happiness all the time is not strictly accurate, as there have sometimes been some very unhappy people in the team, who have lost their "partner" to another hospital radio member.

It would not be sensible of me to list all the "pairings", as this would also require a list of the "partings". So diplomatically only Jane and Mike have been mentioned. The list however of pairings and partings would be very, very long.

On a happier note it is always amusing to see the wonderful aura of the "bubbly" presenter in the studio or out on a public address gig, being "lusted" after by the "dour" backroom engineer types (and sometimes the other way round!)

The attraction of opposites makes the world go round and at hospital radio, over the years, we have managed to have a complete spectrum of opposites working together. Perhaps that is what makes it such a pleasant group to belong to.

We have never been very successful in arranging large gatherings of members for socials or dances, but small groups from time to time have always had fun together. Perhaps the most well-documented of these "gatherings" has been shown at the Southampton Carnival.

Here the technical wizards get their act together and for many years we had a scaffolding commentary box set up outside the United Reform Church in the Avenue (just at the entrance to the Common).

The presenters would visit the floats and entries whilst they were being marshalled for the parade, so that when they passed our location they could talk at some length about the construction of the floats and about the people on board them.

Occasionally HBA entered our own float and the photographs do not really display the hundreds of hours of effort that went into organising and building them.

In the 1970's and again in the 1990's we were the beneficiaries of some of the proceeds distributed by the Southampton Carnival Committee.

Dressing-up for the carnival and parading through the city has always been a good way to put hospital radio's name in the press and great fun for the participants involved. Unfortunately, it is difficult to find the energy, and a big enough team of volunteers, to build and enter a float, when everyone has already devoted a huge amount of their spare time to the radio station.

Mike Smith and Jane Baron, who met at HBA were married in 1977. Two of the very long serving team of outside broadcasters. Both are still very active members and now bring their grown up daughter and son along on many of the gigs.

Carnival Entry 1972
Back row standing: Marie Fielder, Ken Holloway, Lynn Hitchcock, Ann Tupper, Guy Garrett, Barbara Bond and Friend.
Seated front: Miss Lyn Tupper, Robin Kay and Tim Marshall.

Promoting the Programme: "Down at HBA Arms" - photographed at King George Pub, Oakley Road, (just down the road from our studio).
Left to right: Paula Woodward, Graham Fielder, Ron Fitton, Mark Woodward, Phillip Rioch, Julian Boast, Alan Lambourn.

Carnival capers 1973 left to right Chris Smith, Barbara Bond, Marie Fielder, Mark Bowen, Lynn Hitchcock, Eric Thompson, Lesley Wellman and Guy Garrett.

Carnival 1973 advertising our telephone number.
Not the number to call for this "nurse" (Guy Garrett in drag)

Carnival Float 1976 featuring Ray Gatehouse, Mark Bowen, Ric Bailey, Barry West, Colin Chaffers, John Grove and a few others in disguise.

Martin Dale (left) and James Dale (no relation) with the outside broadcast caravan at The Avenue United Reform Church watching the 1976 Carnival Procession. This event was broadcast live back to the studio by a BT line which was strung over the roof of the Church, across the Avenue, and then run all the way down Northlands Road to connect to our permanent tie-line from the County Ground.

Carnival Float 1976

Part of the duties for Pete Phillips at the 1976 carnival was to interview some of the participants as they passed by. This job is affectionately known as "the man in the gutter with the microphone" not an easy task.

The outside broadcast crew at the 1976 Southampton Carnival.
Left to right: Jan Dale, Val Ash, Jim Dale, Clive John, Mike Smith, Syd Wilson, Robin Kay.
(Not forgetting the studio team at home base.)

Gwladys Evans and Bob Crates reporting from their scaffold eyrie outside the Avenue
United Reform Church as the 1978 Southampton Carnival passes by.

"The Radiolettes" an HBA entry in the 1980 Southampton Carnival: including Alan Lambourn, Phil Smith, Colin Ryde, Ken Holloway, Trevor Humphrey, Mike Castle, Tony Rees, Colin Briggs and Malcolm Wright.

The 1981 Carnival, outside the The Avenue United Reform Church, using two OB caravans and the scaffold tower enabling the commentators to be above the crowd.

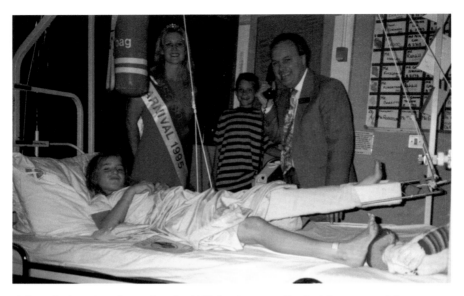

A live telephone broadcast when the 1995 Southampton Carnival Queen toured the Children's Wards at Southampton General.
Katrina Alexander (in bed), Karen Oakley - Carnival Queen and Alan Crowther, a patient, looking on.
From the telephone in the Wards Roy Stubbs linked up with the studio so that the children's requests and interviews with Karen were broadcast live throughout the hospital network.

Carolyn Blake organised a huge team to participate in the 1996 Southampton Carnival. The publicity is wonderful but the effort is a great strain on a team of volunteers who already commit a large part of their spare time to the radio station.

Alan Lambourn and Chris Litton in the control room caravan for the 1992 Carnival, parked outside the Avenue Church.

The route of the Carnival changed and no longer ended at Southampton Common. Our vantage point moved to the Guildhall Square where we could link up with our Guildhall tie-line. For this 1995 event Sue Dumont and Rob Colborne were the commentators with Tim Dale in charge of sound control. They were perched high on a scaffold tower and Bertha was in the background. This project required around a dozen volunteers to make it happen - obviously not all of them are in the photograph.

CHAPTER 13

Outside Broadcasts
1964 to 2002

Studio programmes were supplemented by regular live outside broadcasts via the GPO line network, bringing in not only football and cricket commentaries, but also entertainment and social events from central Southampton venues. These were often transmitted live to the patients receiving our programmes, bringing a taste of life outside the confines of their hospital beds, to relieve the tedium of their stay in hospital.

The very first outside recording for Hospital Radio was made by Geoff Allcock in October 1964, at the Church when Maureen and John Stranger were married, and the tape was later played on the air. Geoff and his wife Mary were there as well as Ken Flood and his wife Doreen.

The first official musical recording by the engineering crew was "Showboat" from the Gaumont Theatre also in October 1964 and played as an edited tape to the patients.

By December 1964 the engineers were becoming more adventurous. They recorded children singing Carols in their school hall as well as the grown-up Carol singers around the Christmas Tree in the Civic Centre forecourt. A special Christmas message from the mayor, plus personal messages from friends and relatives were also pre-recorded. The whole package then edited into magnificent taped programmes, which were broadcast over the Christmas holiday. This was obviously well-received, as in appreciation, a donation of 5 shillings was received from a grateful patient.

Maureen Stranger, using a lip mike borrowed from the football section, recorded the first religious programme from Bitterne Roman Catholic Church. She recorded the Sunday Morning Mass on to a tape and this recording was later broadcast.

The Nursing staff at RSH presented a pantomime at the Chantry Hall in January 1965. This was recorded and subsequently played over the air.

In May 1965 the engineers purchased a new portable tape-recorder at a cost of £50.00 and produced edited folk music recordings made at the Concorde Club. A performance of Iolanthe by the Southampton Operatic Society at the Guildhall was also recorded.

These engineering adventures, as shown in the minutes, were so successful that the enthusiastic team then proposed to record the Southampton Carnival, the Regatta and the Festival of Flowers.

As it was not practical to invite visitors to the underground studios, outside recordings became a very important feature to the programme schedules.

The £17.00 fee for a GPO line from the 1965 Southampton Show on the common to our studio was considered to be too expensive, particularly as it could not be guaranteed that listeners would be able to hear their requests played during the day on the Rediffusion system.

However, in August 1965, a commentary of the Southampton Carnival was broadcast live, using a specially rented line connected directly from our commentary position in the Avenue to the Rediffusion centre.

By 1969, outside broadcasting was becoming "old hat" and they were even going abroad. The Saturday Night Out team of Alan Lambourn, Dallas Stone and Sonya Garrett went across the Channel to LeHavre and recorded their "In-Tune" programme on board the Ferry.

One of the long-running outside events in the late 1960's was a school quiz show called, "That's a Good Question", which saw fierce competition amongst the young contestants representing 19 local secondary schools and from a technical point of view it was a major achievement. Perhaps the most significant event was the silencing of the Civic Centre Clock for three hours. In July 1969 the City demanded a fee of £2.10 for the clock engineer to climb the tower to stop the chimes whilst the recording of the finals of the quiz were taking place in the Southampton Guildhall.

In January 1970 Bonhomie paid £200 for the purchase of an Eccles Avenger Caravan for HBA to use as an Outside Broadcast support vehicle. This was fitted-out by the engineers as a complete mobile studio with mixers, microphones and tape-decks and set-up for its inaugural event on 19th November 1970 when HRH The Duchess of Kent opened the new Radiography Unit at the Royal South Hants hospital.

The mobile station first went on-air at 11.57am and with a direct line to the Rediffusion network we broadcast a four-hour live programme.

Taped music had been pre-recorded as "fillers" with many live interviews throughout the day, as well as a few interviews that had been pre-recorded in the days prior to the event.

At one point Alan Lambourn was given a portable tape recorder and told to "follow the Duchess everywhere"; he was, however, stopped at the entrance door to the ladies cloakroom, but as a serious radio presenter, he continued his running commentary without a skip on the tape.

As with all OB's there is a great deal of setting-up and dismantling, requiring hundreds of yards of cables to be run out and then coiled back up again at the end. Andrew Newton, one of the engineers, cut his head open at this gig and had to attend the casualty ward for stitches. All was well however, and he did not need a request played for him.

The mobile caravan unit extended the locations we were able to broadcast from in the years ahead. The GPO lines from the Guildhall and Mayflower were in regular use and when the Saints were playing away, commentaries from the away team hospital radio were regularly supplemented by our own commentators' remarks whilst visiting the games. There were even a couple of commentaries from Wembley Stadium via a rented GPO line.

When the FM wavelengths were made available in the 1980's the OB team often applied for a 24 hour broadcast licence and transmitted back to our studio from their mobile unit. This was the innovation brought in by James Dale, using his own broadcasting equipment. Jim joined hospital radio in 1974 and his wife Jan joined two years later, and the OB team was also strengthened when their children Tim and Sarah joined the crew.

James led the team through many technological innovations to bring in a superb broadcast, or if it could not be broadcast live, his team recorded dozens of really first-class concerts, choirs and musical extravaganzas from all sorts of locations. Beaulieu Abbey, Romsey Abbey, St Mary's Church, local Schools and Church Halls by the dozen.

In the past few years, now that we have the ISDN connections his team have broadcast crystal clear programmes live from the Southampton Carnival, Turner-Sims, and Romsey Abbey, as well as from Southampton Guildhall and the Mayflower.

ISDN connections are now also used to broadcast the sports commentaries from the Hampshire Rose Bowl and from Friends Provident St Mary's.

In 2001 the OB team broadcast over 26 live events. James and Janice Dale have been supported throughout the years by Graham Lines who joined hospital radio in 1968, and Jane and Mike Smith who joined in 1972 and 1975 respectively. Eric Moore, a member since 1988, and Alex Tame, a relative newcomer who has only been with the team for 5 years, who between them form a really formidable core team, regularly supplemented by other HBA members to assist with the commentating.

When a presenter joins the OB team to "do the talking" on any gig they are always overwhelmed by the efficiency and technological superiority they meet when they turn up.

The OB team members are usually at the site hours and hours before the start, and often do not leave until many hours after the broadcast, with some early arrivals and late departures being made through rear windows of the buildings. Fun and technical expertise has always been the watchword for the outside broadcast team.

"Road Shows" have been organised from the lawn in front of the General Hospital and a few times from the bandstand in the Marlands Shopping centre. Here the PA team and the OB teams combine their efforts but the difficulty here is to combine a programme of events that would amuse the live crowd at the venue and also be good radio for the listeners in the hospitals. This has been found to be a difficult mixture to achieve. For the engineers and presenters these events have always been great fun, but as a quality broadcast event, and as a fundraiser, they have not been terribly successful.

The marquee at the 1972 Southampton Show on the Common, with the first Outside Broadcast Caravan on display and members selling draw tickets to passers by. Good for PR but not a financial success.

Inside the Southampton Show marquee with left to right: Barry West, Chris Pointer, Phil Smith and Val Ash at the mixer desk preparing for live transmission.

Mike Smith, Graham Lines, Tim Dale, Jan Dale and Alex Tame (Jim Dale took the photo), setting up for a live broadcast, beamed from the roof of Romsey Abbey in 1995, with the aid of a 24 hour radio transmission licence.

Jim Dale, Jan Dale and Mike Smith recording a choral event at Beaulieu Abbey in 1991.

Andy Barnes, Graham Lines, Jan Dale and Ken Fielder broadcasting live from the basement below the stage at the Mayflower Theatre in 1997. The commentary is made possible by the use of a video camera set up at the front of the stage, relaying the scene "below stairs" where we have our control centre.

Graham Lines, Ken Fielder and Jan Dale broadcasting live from the commentary box at the side of the stage "one floor up" at Southampton Guildhall in 1998.

CHAPTER 14
Football Section
1964 to 2002

Throughout the past 50 years we have broadcast almost every home game played by the Saints, and in the 1960's and 1970's many away games were also broadcast as well.

Away broadcasts were arranged by connecting a GPO line from, say, Norwich to our local Southampton GPO network, and then we would broadcast the live Norwich hospital radio commentary to the Southampton hospital listeners.

Sometimes our lads would go to the away game and sit alongside the local hospital broadcasting team, and interject with their comments. Entrance to football games was always free, as most football clubs are supportive of hospital radio.

Sometimes the away team hospital broadcasting commentators would turn-up at Southampton and we would give them a 15-minute timeslot within our commentary. Sometimes, the Southampton commentary would be supplied to the away team's hospital broadcasting network by them connecting their hospital radio studio, via a GPO line, to our studio desk.

Up to 1973 we broadcast a game almost every week not only the first team home matches, but if we were not able to connect with the away game, then we would broadcast the local Reserves match.

Broadcasting away matches stopped in the 1980's because of the huge increase in the BT line rental charges.

Leslie Sullivan started the broadcasts sitting on his own, but soon realised that he needed help, particularly after one broadcast which lasted four hours due to the floodlights failing. The game was delayed for a couple of hours whilst repairs were carried out and aided only by the light from his pipe, Sully continued to talk to the patients for the whole time the line was open. There were no musical interludes to fall back on at that time.

Sully was initially joined at The Dell by N.K.Bean (Inky) and also by Frank Le Druillenec. Ken Flood was promoted from sitting on the steps with the control unit, into Inky's seat, in 1960.

For the next ten years the trio then became Sully, Ken and Frank, however when Frank moved to Exeter, in 1971, the third seat was then shared between Bryan Dowding and Ken Fielder, two of the regular members of the Association.

When Sully retired from his commentary role in 1977 the trio, in the three free seats at The Dell, became Ken Flood, Ken Fielder and Bryan Dowding.

This trio still hold their positions today and have now clocked up over 100 years of football commentating between them.

The football club have again given us three seats at its new ground at St Mary's and also provide us with an ISDN telephone connection point. Our commentators sit with the mixer on their lap and share two microphones between them, plus a third is set up on a stand for background effects.

From the mixer there is a hard wire connection down to the two Induction Loop areas, located at each end of the stadium, to provide the home and away partially-sighted supporters with our commentary.

Throughout the years the Southampton Football Club have been incredibly supportive of our service and particular thanks must be given to the board of directors and the senior members of staff for this continuing support.

When we started our broadcasts in 1952, Ted Bates, who had joined Southampton as a 19 year-old in 1937, had just been promoted to Head Coach. Ted became the manager in 1955 and the team at that time were at the bottom of Division 3 (South). When he handed over the manager's job in 1973 they had risen through the ranks and were now in Division 1.

Through these same years the coverage of the hospital radio broadcasts expanded. From just two hospitals in the beginning, the service was now being relayed to ten different locations.

The public's demand for football commentaries by the year 2002 has also grown, with full commentaries now being provided by BBC local radio and also by a local commercial radio station, as well as by us. Nevertheless we still like to feel that our service is personal and friendly and our commentators know who their listeners are, and try to make sure their reports keep the supporters who cannot be at the ground, fully informed.

40 years after the first commentary in 1952, the hospital radio football team met for a Celebration Dinner at The Dell in October 1992.

In the back row is veteran Saints star Ted Bates, who signed on as the Saints Coach in 1952, and Bryn Elliott who played wing half for the Saints in Leslie Sullivan's very first commentary, when they drew 3 all with Doncaster Rovers. The three commentators in the front row are (left to right) Ken Fielder, Bryan Dowding and Ken Flood.
(Photograph courtesy of Southampton Daily Echo)

The 40th Celebration held at The Dell.
Sitting in the Trainers Dugout left to right: Bryan Dowding, Ken Fielder, Audrey Sullivan, Ken Flood, Bryn Elliott, Geoff Allcock, Maureen Stranger and John Stranger.

Dedicated trio: Ken Flood (left), Bryan Dowding (centre) and Ken Fielder.

Saturday 22nd April 2000, when Saints were at home to Manchester United marked the celebration of the 1000th hospital radio commentary of a league match from The Dell. Ken Flood (left) with Bryan Dowding and Ken Fielder warming up their tonsils to begin their performance. At the ages of 76, 68 and 69 respectively, between them they have put in over 100 years service to Southampton Hospital Radio.

The three football commentators at the new Friends Provident St Mary's ground in October 2001, learning how to use the new ISDN equipment, with Jim Dale giving the instructions. Notice the wonderful seating arrangements.

One of the guests on the Roy Stubbs weekly "Roundabout" programme was Lawrie McMenemy.

Daily Mirror

EUROPE'S BIGGEST DAILY SALE

6p   Wednesday, April 28, 1976   ✦   ✦   ✦   No. 22,471

SILENCE IS MISERY..

BED-RIDDEN patients in nine hospitals have been barred from hearing the F A Cup Final on radio.

Wembley officials say they cannot find room for two commentators who want to broadcast to patients on a special G P O line.

The commentators are part of a team which broadcasts all Southampton's home and away

By ALAN GORDON

matches to the hospitals.

Last night, Brian Dowding, vice-chairman of the Southampton and Winchester Hospital Broadcasting Association said : " Dozens of seriously-ill patients will be deprived of their team's greatest hour."

Fitter patients will be

able to reach hospital T V sets to watch the match, he said.

But many will be unable to leave their beds. They wil not hear the B B C commentary because the hospital radio receivers are tuned mainly to V H F and the match was not being broadcast on that frequency.

Portable radios were banned by the hospital,

Southampton Hospital Radio makes the front page of a National Newspaper.

CHAPTER 15
Cricket Section
1966 to 2002

In the early 60's John Stranger was a regular at the Hampshire Cricket ground and talked at great length about the new hospital radio music section and of course about the football commentaries that had become well established.

There were no cricket commentaries at that time and the cricket club agreed that if we provided a "garden shed" we could perch it on top of the flat roofed single storey administration block. So HBA bought a shed and access was via a ladder from the gent's toilet. This accommodated three people.

Commentating began originally on 30th July 1966 from this shed, but after a couple of seasons our benefactor Norman Olden paid for a new commentary box to be erected. This was some fifteen feet off the ground on a scaffold tower, at the Northlands Road end of the Ground "behind the bowlers arm" and there were complaints from residents in Northlands Road that we had spoiled their view down the wicket.

Some of the early volunteer commentators were Major Rupert Robinson, Desmond Eagar and Bill Shepheard. The manager of The Polygon Hotel, Jimmy Woods, was also a regular commentator, but his portly stature, which increased over the years, was not compatible with the access to the new commentary box - a wobbly builder's ladder and a shed door which opened outwards!

Later, a brick plinth replaced the scaffolding, with access via an exterior wooden staircase. In the gales of 1987 the bowler's sightscreens at the club were destroyed and the replacements at the start of the 1988 season were constructed much higher than before. (There were now bowlers on the circuit standing at 6'8" tall.)

The calamity was that the new sight-screens blocked the view from our commentary position so we had to raise the level of the box. This was done by a builder laying six courses of bricks on top of the existing wall and he achieved this by "jacking up" each corner, one brick at a time. A wonderful achievement as the original plans were to hire a crane to lift "the box" which would have probably imploded in the process. This extra height was the subject of numerous planning problems, but a successful outcome was achieved and a cheque for £200 from The League of Friends at The General paid for the construction materials.

The first commentary "team leader" was Major Rupert Robinson, followed by Jim Saunders and then John White. John Young later joined the commentary team and has now been responsible for organising the commentator's roster for over 25 years. This season he has to fill over 700 thirty-minute commentary slots at the Rose Bowl and his telephone will be red-hot trying to co-ordinate the dozens of volunteers.

A few of the early commentators who have helped have included Freddie Odds, Charlie Knott, Bill Stevens and Ronnie Nelson.

When Hampshire were playing at Dean Park, Bournemouth, the commentating team would assemble in the small green hut alongside the main press box. A GPO line would then connect the volunteers to the Southampton studio and the broadcast would be transmitted around the Southampton hospital network.

Ken Maxted, who lives in Bournemouth was the Dean Park cricket booking agent and is still one of the "long serving" volunteer commentators on the hospital radio cricket team. He was very actively involved with the Bournemouth commentaries when Hampshire used their ground from 1978 through to 1992.

The county boundaries changed in 1974 and Bournemouth "moved" out of Hampshire into Dorset, but most of the cricket fans in the Bournemouth area still recognise Hampshire as their home team, because Dorset doesn't have a County Side.

Hampshire stopped playing at Dean Park when their lease expired in 1992, however the ground is still used quite extensively now as the sports and cricket ground for Bournemouth University.

Commentating on cricket matches is an acquired skill and requires the ability to keep talking whilst there is apparently nothing happening in front of your eyes to comment upon. When a cricket personality comes into the commentary box for an interview, it is like receiving a birthday present. (You never quite know what is in the package, but you are delighted to receive it.)

In 1977 at the County Ground when Hampshire were playing Gloucestershire, Ken Maxted, who was alone in his box at the top of the scaffolding tower, was describing Hampshire's batting skills, felt the box move when someone ascended the ladder. Ken assumes it was his relief commentator and carried on his commentary. Glancing round five minutes later he recognised Barry Richards, arguably, one of the most exiting batsmen in the game, sitting next to him. A 20-minute interview followed, which was fortunately captured on tape by Alan Lambourn, the man at the Winchester Road studio control desk.

At the end of the interview, with the microphone switched off, Ken thanked Barry for taking so much of his valuable time to visit our commentary box, and Barry said, "This is the BBC isn't it?" Ken's reply hit him like an Andy Robert's bouncer, he had been booked (and probably been paid an enormous sum) for a 30 minute BBC interview at their box which was at the other end of the Ground. HBA had yet another scoop, and to this day it is still rumoured to be the only free interview that the great cricketer ever gave.

In the annuls of cricketing history it has been recorded that the County Ground is most unusual as it has two commentary boxes: "one for the BBC and one for less-fortunate listeners in hospital". It was later mentioned that this was not a comment on the commentaries provided by the stalwart team of hospital radio volunteers.

Commentating at a cricket match is obviously live and the commentator must be on his mettle to keep the listeners informed and entertained. A few years ago John Young was at the microphone when the Indian National Team were playing at Southampton. The incoming batsman was not the one pre-printed on the scorecard, and the large scoreboard on the other side of the ground was more confused than he was. It didn't help that despite his many years as a cricket commentator and his amazing memory for names, half the Indians he had never seen before and the other half had unpronounceable names, and to add to the confusion they all wore helmets and visors. You can imagine the state he was in.

The telephone beside him rang - a message from the studio about the tea break interval plans - a wasp persistently buzzed around the back of his neck (it actually stung him on this occasion) and a " friendly" member of HBA lifted one of his earphones, thus dislodging his glasses, to tell him "Here is Sunil Gavaskar, I've managed to get him up for an interview for you" - and he was still "live on air".

When you are going to interview someone it is usually prudent to prepare some notes and to have some idea about the way to make the interviewee happy to respond, and to make the conversation enjoyable to the listeners. Preparation is the key! What a hope - John was in it - and his memory came up with the point that not only was Gavaskar a brilliant batsman, but he could also bowl. John mentioned his bowling expertise and asked him to recall the Test wicket he had bowled. Sunil replied " I did take out Zaheer Abass, playing for Pakistan, when he had scored 100 in the first innings, and I was brought on when he had scored 96 in the second. The Indians then called in their secret weapon - that's me - to get him out. I sent down a leg spinner and the great man was out - at 96 - a glorious event, Zaheer was always confident of scoring at least 100 every time he went in. Here today I hope all your listeners soon get better and tell them to stay tuned for a repeat performance of the Indian team's secret weapon. I will be back after tea to send all your Hampshire boys back to the Pavilion". With that he was off to the Pavilion for his cucumber sandwiches and John handed back to the studio, where they played music in the tea interval, whilst John rubbed his sore neck and ate his own cucumber and salmon sandwiches.

Other interviewees who have graced our commentary box have included: John Arlott, Henry Blofeld, Terry Wogan, Bill Frindall, Greg Chappell and also Lee McKenzie who was an HBA member for about a year, before he became a professional broadcaster.

Part of the efficiency of a cricket commentary is due in no small part to the efforts of "the scorer". This expertise is in a field of its own. The scorers down the years have included Jim Pook, Andrew Murray, Brian Scotson, Peter Andrews and Roy Scott. Their huge chart of information, lovingly maintained throughout the day, is an absolutely essential tool for the man doing the talking. When nothing is happening on the field a quick scan of the scorer's numbers immediately gives him fuel for his chatter.

For well over 30 years we have been bringing to our listeners ball-by-ball commentaries every summer, which have kept our commentating team on their toes. Until the mid 1990's there was a logistics problem, as an engineer was required to visit the studio to switch off our regular music programmes, so that the cricket commentaries could take over. However Phil Soper designed a telephone switching system enabling them to dial-up the studio from their telephone line at the ground and, by entering a secret code, could take command of the airwaves. This enabled the cricket team to go live direct from the County Ground and to switch back to the 24-hour programme schedule whenever they had finished. The wonders of technology!

With the move from the County Ground to the new Hampshire Rose Bowl there have been two significant changes. On the one hand the connection is now made using a digital ISDN telephone line, dramatically improving the quality of the broadcasts, and secondly almost a doubling of the quantity of cricket now being available, with Bournemouth, Portsmouth and Basingstoke matches all being consolidated into the one location. The first evening match was also such a roaring success that no doubt there will be more of these in the future. The accommodation for our commentators at the new ground however, still leaves room for improvement, as we have been operating from a temporary portacabin, but we anticipate being given a space in their new "media centre" when it is built.

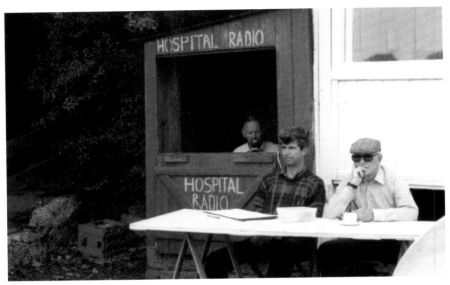

The pre-war telephone hut at Dean Park, Bournemouth in 1992 with John Young doing the commentating inside, with only spiders and ivy for company, whilst Ronnie Nelson (in the hat) kept the score.

The comments from the excited crowd at Dean Court would be picked up by the "effects microphone" fitted above the door of our commentary hut.

An artist's impression of our commentary box on the scaffold tower, with it's ladder at the rear, situated alongside Northlands Road at the County Ground

Our modernised commentary box now supported by a brick plinth at the now evacuated Southampton County Ground.

Some of the team, who enjoyed a free entry to watch the cricket in the summer of 2000, but had to spend hours talking about it. From the top: Claud Carter, Peter Andrews, Ken Maxted, Rob Colborne (Secretary of HBA) John Young (Cricket Co-ordinator) and Roy Scott (scorer).

Roy Scott on the left keeping score and John Young keeping the listeners entertained from the County Ground Commentary Box. Note the sophisticated "effects mike".

When the TV crew arrive, and they use a white ball, our commentary box is shrouded in black. In a recent world series match the Sky TV crew completely blocked our view with their scaffolding.

In 1995 the outside broadcast team were called to the County Ground to install a new power supply cable. This required an 18" channel about 100 yards long. This took two days to complete and the crew on this day included left to right: Jan Dale, Phil Soper, Ken Fielder, Graham Lines, Ivor Worsley, Ken Flood, Nick Smith, Adrian Wint, Jim Dale, Eric Moore and Mike Smith.

CHAPTER 16

Winchester (WHR)

1968 to 1984

In April 1968 the first connection to The County Hospital Winchester was made, but it was not until 12th October 1968 that the first programmes were transmitted down the line from the Southampton studio.

St Paul's was later connected to the system on 3rd July 1970. An item in the press quoted " The service to St Paul's began last Friday and requests started to come in on Saturday morning".

Funds for the £6000 Winchester installation covering the wiring network and handsets in the wards as well as the FM receivers, were kindly provided by Winchester League of Friends.

In the early stages of our Winchester connection we only paid for the time we were using the GPO line, but later we installed permanent lines where we paid an annual fee and thus ensured our Winchester listeners received continuous programmes from our Southampton studio.

These permanent line charges were to be a serious drain on our resources in the ensuing years.

Initially the Association was known as Southampton and Winchester Hospital Broadcasting but, during the early 1980's, two events occurred which led to the separation of the Winchester Hospital Radio Station (WHR) as a self-contained unit.

Firstly Carole Line, a member of Southampton Hospital Radio who lived in Winchester, was approached by Idwal Wheale at the Royal Hampshire County Hospital with a view to improving the contact between HBA and the Winchester Hospital's patients. Secondly Southampton HBA were struggling to meet the costs of their extensive annual GPO landline bills, the Winchester connection being quite a significant component thereof.

Steve Feeney and Tony Knight, members of Southampton Hospital Radio, and who lived in Winchester and, by coincidence, happened to be part of the Tuesday evening crew, got together a plan to set up a separate Hospital Radio Station exclusively for the Winchester Hospitals.

In association with Jeremy Fermo, a Winchester businessman, they put together a plan which was approved by the Southampton HBA Executive committee. Then, with the support of the Winchester hospital management, who provided a couple of rooms on the second floor of a building at the rear of St Paul's Hospital, they were in business.

Winchester City Lottery provided a grant for £3,500 which covered the major part of the project costs, but it took more than a year to design and build the studios and to raise the rest of the funding before they were able to go live on 24th September 1984.

These rooms, however, proved to be far too small to cope with training, recording or any other expansion plans and maintenance was a nightmare. More space was not readily available until the County Hospital found them a dilapidated building with holes in the roof and outside walls, containing old toilet cubicles and jammed full with surplus hospital equipment.

From this dismal building, with a very intensive campaign to raise the £40,000 costs, there grew two back-to-back sound studios, a record library, an engineering room (such luxury) a conference room and a kitchen/ social room.

Winchester Hospital Radio (WHR) went live from their new studio premises on 6th June 1992 when Bert Weedon performed their opening ceremony and they have continued to go from strength to strength, with a 24 hour radio service now on the horizon and Patientline also about to be installed.

At Southampton, up to 1983 Tony Knight had been presenting a weekly chat show on Tuesday evenings called "Roundabout". At that time I presented the "Country from the Western" programme on the same evening and I had also been standing in for Tony Knight on his 60 minute chat show whenever he could not make it. From 1983 however I was promoted, full time, to this weekly interview programme, and I have now been meeting guests on Tuesday evenings for almost 20 years.

SOUTHERN EVENING ECHO, Friday, September 24, 1982

HOSPITAL RADIO IS HIT BY PHONE COSTS

"GROTESQUE AND CRUEL" price increases by British Telecom will kill off Southampton's popular hospital broadcasting service unless top level action is taken, Southampton Itchen MP Bob Mitchell has been warned.

Alarming and frequent price rises for vital music lines will cripple Southampton and Winchester HBA in two years, says station manager Mr. Alan Lambourn.

"We are being unfairly punished by British Telecom for providing sick people with pleasure," he said.

Mr. Lambourn sent a warning letter to Mr. Mitchell who has passed it to the Minister concerned. He has now asked him to have talks

By Staff Reporter

with British Telecom about the problem.

HBA rents seven lines including outside broadcasting points such as the Dell, County Ground and Guildhall. This will cost £5,580 in December.

Mr. Lambourn said: "In the next rental year and for the ensuing five years the cost of these lines will have risen by 50 per cent. By 1987 a rise in excess of 2,000 per cent will have been recorded."

The voluntary service — which puts programmes out to 11 hospitals — was forced to abandon line coverage of this year's Southampton Show when faced with a £1,000 connection charge between the Common and the studio centre at the Western Hospital.

"This connection charge has increased from £60 to £200 per line and rises further when VAT appears. That is 233 per cent within one year ..." he added.

British Telecom's continual price rises had meant the closure of two HBA stations and the decline of several others, said Mr. Lambourn.

Hospital broadcasting was vital for the mental well-being of patients. It often led to "unbelievable" improvement in patient's progress, he added.

A British Telecom spokesman said the matter was now "sub judice" until the meeting with the Minister. But he added: "Even for charitable organisations we have no mandate for discounts".

Newspaper clipping illustrating why Southampton were happy to see Winchester set up on their own.

CHAPTER 17
Public Address Unit
1984 to 2000

In 1984 Southampton University were offered a London Weekend Television outside broadcast vehicle, a Bedford Box Van, which was surplus to their requirements. Colin Ryde, a student and HBA member, heard of this offer and suggested this would be a wonderful asset for the HBA outside broadcasting team and the University were happy to step aside for us.

This was the start of a whole new era of fund-raising activity and had a major impact on the public's awareness of Southampton Hospital Radio. Formerly, the outside broadcasting team had used only a small caravan, equipped to operate as a mobile studio, which was towed to the outside broadcast site. For a couple of years HBA owned a Landrover, purchased from the Army, but this proved to be uneconomic. It only cost £400 to purchase and was sold two years later for £200 so was not a capital item of expense, but maintenance and repair costs in relation to its usage was a financial burden.

Initially there was some concern raised by the executive committee that we were taking on a huge vehicle, representing a liability we could not afford, having some years earlier experienced the Landrover maintenance troubles.

The team of Ken Holloway, Val Ash and Peter Phillips had already been fund-raising for a few years by offering a Public Address facility to local fetes and charity events. They had used the outside broadcast caravan and also worked from their private cars, and were quite convinced this new vehicle would be a significant money-making project.

The public address services they provided would be rewarded with a donation to HBA. The volunteers would organise the outdoor charity events at a price less than half they would otherwise pay to commercial firms. After all there were no staff wages to pay - all the personnel were HBA volunteers - and the running costs of keeping the vehicle on the road were not too onerous, as it was only used at the weekends.

Fitting out the vehicle took almost two years of devoted effort by the HBA members. As well as Ken, Val and Peter the engineering expertise of Phil Soper and Ivor Worsley was again called into service, assisted by Chris Litton and Ken LeLievre, these members put in many hundreds of hours to build this mobile studio.

However in 1986, the first full year it was in service performing public address gigs, it achieved an income of almost £2,000. Thereafter the annual income from PA's averaged around £7,000 except for 1994 when it raised over £8,500 in one year.

Over the years, from 1986 to the year 2000 (when the vehicle was scrapped) the PA unit earned in total over £82,000 in donations, against total running costs of only £20,000 (See Appendix A)

The Public Address team were out almost every weekend in the summer months. Local charities who ran Fetes and Fairs called on our services and they normally booked the team at the end of a gig for the same event the following year. The presenters were all skilled not only in their ability to pass along serious messages to the crowds, but also they were able to "jolly along" the proceedings. The rigging crew who had the worst job had to be at the event long before it started and were usually the last to leave having de-rigged at the end of the day.

Some events were very complex, for example the Poole Marathon needed four commentary locations consisting of two separate start points, a finish point and an awards ceremony point. This gig therefore used not only "Bertha" but also two caravans as well, and as the Competitors started their run at 9am we had to be on site (at Poole) at 7.30am - on a Sunday Morning - such devotion to duty. For this we received a £400 donation.

In 1999 there were 23 events covered by the Public Address team. Apart from Poole they helped run Marathons and Fun Runs at Basingstoke, Andover, Hook, New Forest, Totton and at Eastleigh for Norwich Union. In addition they also attended and supported shows and exhibitions at Eastleigh, Isle of Wight, Stubbington, Baddesley, Durley, Fenwick Hospital, Southampton Sports Centre and even made a few School events go with a swing.

As you can imagine with dozens of gigs attended every year and over the sixteen years the vehicle was in action there are hundreds of stories to tell of dramas and pain suffered by the participants. The most pain being inflicted by the weather, for winding up hundreds of metres of wet cable back on their drums, at the end of the day, is not fun.

By the time we had arrived in the year 2000 the morale of the Public Address team had already started to wane and there were no new members willing to pick up these activities, leaving the very few remaining HBA team members having to work twice as hard.

Unfortunately the vehicle, parked outside our studio became a magnet to the local vandals so we had to hide it and park it away from the site. This led to operational difficulties as it took ages to load and unload for a gig.

In addition the vehicle only just scraped through it's MOT in 1999 and we were promised only one more year of service from it unless we undertook a serious amount of repair work.

This lead to the disposal in February 2001, of our goose which had laid so many golden eggs for us, for the scrap price of only £200.00. We did strip out the fittings and the equipment and they are now stored in the loft waiting for a new beginning.

The O.B. Caravan, parked outside the studio, was regularly vandalised and in January 2001 it was torched. We claimed on the insurance policy and had to pay for the wreck to be towed away, however this has left us with no outside vehicle at all.

There are sufficient funds available to pay for a replacement Public Address Vehicle, and an OB vehicle, but due to the parking problems, the vandalism, and the lack of enthusiasm from members willing to turn out early on a Sunday morning, it has been agreed that this part of our Association's activities should be temporarily postponed, until more support and enthusiasm from the members could be found.

Many members mourn the loss of the facilities, the loss of the camaraderie that had previously existed in the Public Address team, and most of all, the huge hole that its passing has left in our financial budget. Hopefully this may be resolved sometime in the future.

Paul Duell in his PA Gear ready to roll with "Bertha". Photographed alongside the OB Caravan at the front door of the studio in 1997.

Tim Dale, Jenny Wint and Paul Duell inside the Public Address vehicle when it was being used as the command post for a Carnival. The TV monitors helped locate the roving reporters who would be in the road interviewing the participants. Tim Dale monitoring the radio mikes and Paul controlling the output back to the hospitals.

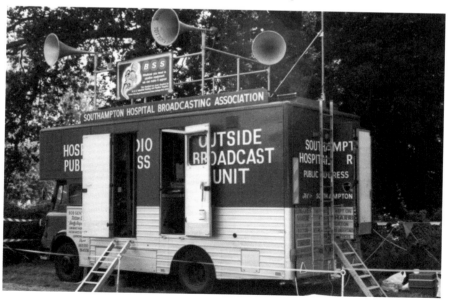

The Public Address vehicle fully dressed and in action earning her keep.

Part of the PA Crew on a 1990 gig left to right Chris Litton, Ken Holloway, Paul Young, Adrian Wint and Ivor Worsley.

Tony Knight (founder of Winchester Hospital Radio) with Colin Ryde at a public address event in 1986.

Ken Holloway, Ivor Worsley and Colin Ryde at the Totton Marathon public address gig in 1986.

Part of the public address team in 1985.
Left to right: Colin Ryde, Ken Holloway, Val Ash, Patrick Shea and Eric Moore.

CHAPTER 18
NAHBO
1970 to 2002

The National Association of Hospital Broadcasting Organisations was formed in 1970 and was born out of the Yorkshire Federation of Tape Recording Clubs.

Many radio stations began by producing their programmes on tape recorders at home and then playing the tape through the hospital's radio system.

Ken Fulstow of Hull, formed firstly, the National Association of Hospital Broadcasting Services Yorkshire, which then became NAHBO in 1970.

Brian Snowden (late husband of the current president June Snowden) was a founder member with Ken, and between them they compiled the first Constitution.

At the inaugural meeting were representatives from Barnsley, Dover, Durham, Edinburgh, Glasgow, Heavy Woollen District, Huddersfield, Hull, Pontefract, Scarborough, Southampton, South Shields and York.

Brian Snowden had been involved in Hospital Radio from the early 60's and met June when she joined York Hospital Radio in 1974 and they both continued their involvement in the National Association, following it through its many development stages down the years.

NAHBO does not produce any radio programmes, but consists of an executive committee who all, in their own right, are involved in hospital radio stations across the country. There are now over 350 member stations in the Association and each station pays a nominal annual subscription for registration.

The newsletter provides a link with like-minded people across the country, for what may be a problem at one radio station may have already been resolved by another. It also represents a national voice when radio licences are being considered and whenever other national problems arise.

When Southampton formed their music section in 1963 they listened to, and learned from, the experiences of Bristol Hospital Radio, and later, when Southampton was moving into the field of computers, a visit to see the Birmingham Hospital Radio computer system in action, was very helpful and informative.

As well as the NAHBO Newsletter helping member stations to keep in touch, there is the national Spring Conference incorporating the BT Awards Ceremony - just like the Oscars in the film world - these NAHBO Awards are highly-prized as national recognition for what is otherwise a local service.

There is also an Autumn Conference each year incorporating the AGM, when the members meet for a long weekend at different Hotels around the UK. The weekend includes seminars, outings to the local stations, and the opportunity for members from all over the country to meet socially and exchange ideas, as well as attending the AGM and voting for the executive positions on the ruling body.

In the formative years this was a less exotic meeting and it is recorded in the Southampton station minutes that we were the hosts for their AGM held over the weekend of 1st and 2nd October 1971. About 30 representatives came from all over the UK, with Saturday being an open day for delegates arriving, then at 10am on Sunday the NAHBO executive met at the General Hospital, followed by a 12.30 luncheon. The group then moved to our studios at 2pm where we entertained them to an interesting afternoon, plus a buffet tea.

Members came from as far away as Paisley and some enjoyed a tour of Southampton whilst they were here.

On the national committee Guy Garrett, the Southampton Station Director, was elected as National Vice Chairman and in that role hoped to influence the Ministry of Post and Telecommunications in obtaining concessions from the GPO line charges. This was not successful and throughout our history both the GPO and later BT have never granted any concessions regarding their charges, to any hospital radio stations.

Guy was also elected to be the national contact with the Ministry of Post and Telecommunications for in the early 70's they were considering issuing a U.H.F. transmission licence, but this never materialised.

In addition to the normal executive committee meetings and the spring and autumn conferences, there is also an important Regional Committee structure, dividing the UK into 9 local regions. We are part of the Southern Region and this enables members from around the South of England to get together to exchange their views and ideas.

The first meeting of the original South and West Region was held at Odstock Hospital Salisbury on 19th November 1972. It was attended by Peter Pritchett-Brown, Marie Ashley-Smith, Bryan Dowding and Allan St. John Holt on behalf of Southampton & Winchester, plus representatives from Bath, Boscombe, Bristol, Chichester, Devizes, Odstock, Portsmouth, and Poole. This was such a successful meeting that a second one was quickly arranged for January 1973 at the same place.

Then on 11th March 1973 the next regional meeting was held at Southampton, allowing us to show-off our new home.

The diversity of the sizes of the various Associations was interesting, with the Southampton service covering ten hospitals, but Bristol were serving 27 hospitals. Boscombe, however, with only two members, no studio, and by using one tape machine compiled, at home, one request programme tape each week.

This same diversity still exists today amongst the radio stations in the UK. With many of the hospitals around the country consolidating their services into huge centralised facilities and many outlying hospitals closing down, this has led to similar consolidations of the hospital radio stations. At one time there were over 700 stations around the country, but they are now reduced to only half that number.

It has been estimated that Hospital Radio across the country, run by over 15,000 volunteers, may arguably be the UK's largest group of unpaid volunteers.

National Hospital Broadcasting Week was celebrated in 1995 when volunteers from Portsmouth Hospital Radio toured the country to demonstrate a special Ambulance for handicapped patients. When it arrived at Southampton we were there to support and broadcast the event. In the vehicle were Portsmouth Hospital Radio members.

Left to right in front, are HBA members Claire Parsonage, Jennifer Wint, Paul Duell and Roy Stubbs.

This event was part of our "Road Show" broadcast live to the patients from a marquee set up on the front lawn of The General Hospital.

Southampton Hospital Radio have won three national awards. Here Graham Fielder, Paul Duell and Sarah Tate collect the 1995 award from Sue Barker at the British Telecom Tower Awards ceremony.

In 1973 Ald. Michael Pettit, The Mayor of Southampton, along with Peter Pritchett-Brown (Chairman) set John Grove (18) off on his 727 mile "Bike Hike" around the hospital radio studios in the South West Region, with the Eastleigh Majorettes cheering him on.
His journey took him via Bournemouth, Poole, Weymouth, Plymouth, up to Bath and Bristol and then into Swansea and back home via Swindon, Basingstoke and Salisbury. Prior to this circular tour he had already visited Portsmouth and the Isle of Wight. At each location he went "on-air" and each station arranged accommodation for him.

In 1982 Peter Berry (Dr. Bogus Berry) and Graham Fielder (Dr. Fancy Free) followed the path previously cycled by John Grove around the Hospital Radio Stations in the South. This time they did it by means of an old ambulance - raising funds for HBA as they enjoyed their "holiday". (Photograph courtesy of Southampton Daily Echo)

CHAPTER 19
The Blind Connection
1980 to 2002

Leslie Sullivan in his role as a member of Toc H was always helping out with the blind members in the community and his initial introduction to football commentating began when he took a blind friend to a football match and kept up a running commentary for him.

At Southampton however, the first association hospital radio had with the blind was the installation of a GPO line to Hillfield Home for the Blind, connected in August 1966.

In 1973 the Talking Newspapers for the Blind were given studio space to record and duplicate their monthly cassettes. Although some of the volunteers for this charity came from the ranks of the HBA team, they were otherwise totally independent of the HBA radio programmes. Their cassettes were increased to a fortnightly turnaround and in recent times they have became a weekly project. Their recording team moved from the prefabricated studio at Bassett, in their formative years, to our first brick built studio at the Chest hospital.

For over 20 years we worked closely with their team, using one of our studios for their weekly recording sessions. However whilst we were negotiating with Tesco for a new studio, they were negotiating at the same time with the developers at the Southampton Centre for the Blind, at Bassett Avenue.

They had now found a permanent home of their own and on 24th Sept 1994 they started recording in their very own purpose-built studio at the Blind Centre at the top of the Avenue. However many of their volunteers still remain as HBA members. With Chris Litton as their chairman and Ivor Worsley as their chief engineer, we still keep very closely in touch with each other.

A totally separate link with the Blind also began in 1973 when we were asked to investigate the possibility of supplying our football commentary to a row of seats at The Dell for blind football supporters. This took quite a few years to organise but by the summer of 1980, Brian Truscott, the Secretary of Southampton Football Club, finalised the negotiations for us to supply a feed of our commentary, to a bench behind the Dugout at the Dell.

In February 1981 our engineers estimated it would cost in excess of £500 to install this cable, but the Southampton Football Club, in association with the Southampton Rotary, found the funds and in the summer of 1981, an additional string was added to the HBA bow, when the cable was installed.

Ten seats were provided, with ten pairs of headphones for blind supporters to enjoy the HBA match commentary.

In a letter dated 23rd May 1982, Ron Fielder, the Vice Chairman of Southampton Society for the Blind, congratulates the three commentators for the 1981-82 football season, stating that "The scheme has given enormous pleasure to many citizens who had previously been unable to appreciate the match atmosphere".

Whilst this service to the local blind supporters was most gratefully received it did create a problem with the transportation of these special supporters. Someone had to collect them from their home and when they arrived at The Dell they needed an escort to their special seats. This exercise was then repeated at the end of the match in order to help them home again.

This problem has been resolved at the new St Mary's ground by a system which allows the blind supporters to sit with their friends and relatives, who can now assist with their personal transport problems and can also sit alongside each other.

In the new stadium at St Mary's the service has been continued, but now the Football Club have installed an induction loop around two areas of seats, so that both the home and the away supporters at the match can benefit. Our running commentary is fed by a direct line into these two induction loop areas and there are eighty seats located within each loop.

This enables the blind and partially deaf supporters to now sit with their friends whilst they enjoy the atmosphere of the match. The football club has paid for this wiring installation and supplies the necessary earpieces for those sitting within the loops.

Left to right: Brian Truscott (Secretary of Southampton Football Club), Alan St John Holt (chairman of HBA) and Ron Townly (Round Table chairman).

Allan is collecting two cheques for £300 each to pay for the installation costs of the wiring to the "blind section" situated behind the trainer's dugout at The Dell.

In 1981 this made Saints the pioneer club for facilities for blind supporters and the Club have continued their support by installing two induction loop circuits in their new stadium at Friends Provident St Marys.

CHAPTER 20

Raising Funds

1952 to 2002

It is interesting to note the Association's changing circumstances over the years but please be aware that inflation distorts the figures quoted.

Initially, from 1952 to 1963 there was the need to fund the GPO line charges and the cost of the few pieces of equipment required to support only the football commentary service. The major source of funds at that time came from the proceeds of an annual friendly game at The Dell plus continuing financial support from the football club management.

However donations were sought and Leslie Sullivan, the creator of our service, worked extremely hard to make sure the bank account never went into the red, by writing continuous begging letters, obviously with some success.

From 1963, when the music section started, a huge change of emphasis in the demand for funds began.

First there was the construction costs for our first studio in the cellars of the Toc H building, plus the purchasing of records, tapes, microphones and recording equipment. The costs of installing and renting the GPO landline charges, however, were always a problem, but quite often a benefactor could be persuaded to meet these in the first year of a new service.

Unfortunately every time a new hospital site was added to the network the GPO recurring annual line charges became an escalating problem.

Leslie Sullivan using his earlier fund-raising contacts worked even harder and his letter-writing became even more prolific

The costs of setting-up the first studios in the basement of Toc H were less than the first estimate of £300 as most of the labouring work was undertaken by the members and the Association only had to purchase the materials.

However the first real studio building erected in 1970 cost almost £9,000 and this was a wooden prefabricated building. This figure did not represent the true cost as once again the members put in many hours of their time in order to decorate and install the central heating, plumbing, electrical wiring and all the internal furnishings and equipment.

The very significant support of the Bonhomie charities were recorded as having contributed £4,000 towards the new studio building as well as donating over £2,000 in previous years, towards the studio running costs.

It is interesting to digress and relate the story of "Bonhomie". The Three Score Club at Junction Road, Totton, had been granted a new lease on their piece of land and wanted to replace their wartime Nissen Hut with a brick building. This was likely to cost over £10,000 and the Southampton Rotarians were called in to help. However the Rotarians wanted to call this special fund-raising activity by a distinct name. A monthly lottery draw was organised and the name chosen was "Bonhomie". After the funds for the initial project had been raised the monthly draw was so popular that in 1963 it was extended to a weekly draw. All the funds raised were then distributed to many local charities. Funds were used to purchase and run, for the disabled, the four famous local minibus vehicles. New community halls were built and new furnishings installed in others. HBA was fortunate to be associated with this fund-raising project and extremely fortunate in having so many Rotarian supporters of our cause. "Bonhomie" funding and their continuing support in later years was really astounding. Leslie Sullivan, as a keen Rotarian, was once again the instigator of much of their largesse and Bill Davis, the manager of Bonhomie, deserves a huge vote of thanks for his support over these very significant years in our history.

Southampton Football Club our very earliest benefactor continued to support our service and it was recorded that over the first 18 seasons from 1952 to 1970 they had donated over £3,000. If this were to be factored-up by inflation, it would probably make their donations well in excess of over £30,000 in today's values.

Other organisations, large and small, that contributed included local Rotary and Inner Wheel Clubs, Toc H branches, Hospital Management Committees,

Leagues of Friends from all the Hospitals served, and many significant donations in our formative years from The Shirley Billiards Club. In total, by 1970, there were over 140 generous financial supporters of HBA.

In 1978 the Association was advised that the Toc H site was being developed for a housing project and a new location for our studios would have to be found. A piece of land on the Chest Hospital site, formerly mentioned some ten years previously, was again offered and Leslie Sullivan's expertise came to the fore. £50,000 was needed to build a replica of the existing building, but this time it was to be constructed in brick and tiles instead of in prefabricated wood sections. The architect Norman Woodford, a Rotarian friend of Leslie Sullivan, once again kindly assisted with the design and planning requirements.

Serious donations were now required and a brief summary of our benefactors included :-

The Football Association	2,000
Bonhomie	8,000
BBC Appeal	
(The Week's Good Cause)	660
Winchester Lottery	8,400
Southampton Pools	1,300
Jubilee Trust	1,000
Hants Area H. Authority	6,000
Southampton City Council	8,000
Eastleigh Borough Council	3,000
Hants County Council	1,000
Test Valley D C	3,000
New Forest R D C	500
General League of Friends	2,000
RSH League of Friends	250
Winchester L of Friends	250
Wade Foundation	750
200 many and varied Donations	
including members Fund-raising	
events over 3 years	8,000

Total = £54,110

The largest room in this building was dedicated with a plaque to Leslie Sullivan, who retired from football commentating in his 70th year in 1977, but continued to work tirelessly for us until he died in 1984.

His plaque was later transferred to the largest room in the new studio building in 1993, so that we still have a "Leslie Sullivan Room" in recognition of his significant contribution to our history.

The new building, the fourth home for the Association opened in 1993, is the subject of a chapter on its own. This time however the members did not have to raise the funds to meet the building costs as our substantial brick building was being demolished at the behest of Tesco, who paid for the construction of the new premises.

Although significant amounts of funds had been raised over the years to meet the studio construction costs it has always been a problem, and still is, for the members to raise funds each and every year to meet the studio running costs.

For example, in the 20 years from 1980 to 2000 we have paid over £96,000 to British Telecom for our telephones and landlines.

Our members' tremendous efforts at raising funds to meet these annual costs are well-recorded, but the number of members participating in fund-raising projects was never enough.

In the three years up to 1969 waste paper collecting was the members' serious fund-raising project and with more than 250 tons collected, this contributed £1,400 to the Association's funds. Waste paper continued to be a source of funds until 1980, but then waste paper prices fell.

From 1970 to 1980 the total studio running costs were around £ 5,000 per annum and the members organised draws and raffles, sold goods at market stalls and continued to collect waste paper. In 1975 there was a charity football match with many stars of stage and screen turning out to support HBA, which raised almost £400.

A Marquee at the Southampton Show each year kept the Association in the public eye and raised many hundreds of pounds. Liz Bryant, who only recently retired after 25 years membership, became the Chief Librarian, but in her earlier years she was noted as being the "great provider of food" at these shows.

Donations from our continuing benefactors at Bonhomie, the various League of Friends' charities and the Hospital Management Committees, made up the shortfalls. Each year it was a struggle to balance the books, but as well as broadcasting a radio service the members kept their financial house in order.

With each move to a new studio building the running costs escalated, in particular the GPO charges in the late 1970's were around £2,000 per annum but by the early 1980's, these had more than doubled to over £5,000 per annum. The cost of the lines to Winchester became a major discussion point and Winchester Hospital Radio broke away and set up their own service.

Members hate fund-raising, but were always willing to try something new and the schedule of events detailed in chapter 21 highlights some of the more significant ones. Ken Holloway's wife Fay, worked in the daytime with Allan St. John Holt, and Ken was persuaded to join HBA to "lend Allan a hand with fund-raising". This was in 1974 and Ken's contribution throughout the past 28 years in the fund-raising department has been quite substantial.

Ken started by organising the tickets for the annual draw and in 1982 he organised, along with Chris Litton, the first of two Army Assault Courses. In 1984, Ken turned his attention to the London Weekend Television vehicle and became responsible for organising the numerous fund-raising Public Address Unit events, until the vehicle was scrapped in 2000, with his wife Fay, regularly turning out to assist him. He has also, since 1987, organised the annual HBA dinner-dance.

Although the Public Address Unit continued to raise a significant part of our running costs it was fairly evident that the many and varied small social gatherings were not very effective as fundraisers, so in the mid 1990's large events were organised. Road Shows were fun for the technical crew, but not wildly successful as fund-raising events. A Balloon Race, followed by Assault Courses in 1995 and 1996 were very successful (A national award from NAHBO was achieved for the 1995 Assault Course event).

From 1994 to 1998 Pauline Soper organised an annual Book Sale or Record Sale at the studio - it usually took a year to sort and price these items, but every event was a huge success. Phil, her husband, although an unpaid helper with her projects, also arranged a couple of second-hand equipment sales days. All goods sold in these events had been donated, and before each sale the upstairs loft was a veritable Aladdin's Cave.

It was evident that, to raise serious funds, it became necessary for other people to assist us, our team was too small and specialised. In 1998 we were successful in placing HBA on the books of HSBC Bank plc as their favoured charity. We had a target to raise £12,000 to meet the cost of the new ISDN equipment for use at the new football and cricket grounds. Both were re-locating in the year 2001 and we had been advised by British Telecom that our old analogue line network around Southampton was about to be terminated.

Many and varied events were organised by the HSBC sports and social club and their 1500 employees were far more efficient at raising funds than we could ever wish to be. However the "coup de grace" was a sponsored Abseil from the roof of the HSBC 14 storey office building in Commercial Road, Southampton and the sponsored abseilers raised almost £18,000 for us.

A complete book could be written about fund-raising at HBA; members hate it with a vengeance, but all the members feel so enthusiastic about the radio station and its essential worth, that they all make an effort to help where they can. See chapter 21 for the financial details of the many and varied fund-raising projects undertaken during the two decades before the turn of the century. This schedule highlights many of the regular events we organised as well as the special events that have been undertaken and the amounts raised by each one.

As a registered charity, raising funds is always the most unpleasant part of volunteering, members who join to operate a radio service, hate the process of fund-raising. However over the years the members of the Association have always managed to keep the bank balance in the black.

I am still looking for the benevolent person who would like to "lend" the Association £250,000 (not give - just lend) and we could have the benefit of the annual interest on this deposit. We would need no further fund-raising activities as the interest on this deposit would meet our annual running costs and the members could then concentrate all their time and energy on improving the programmes. (Anyone can dream)

CHAPTER 21
1981 to 2000

YEAR	Annual Total	Abseil	HSBC	Records / Book Sales	Prize Draws	Tesco / Flag Days	Country & Western	Assault Course	Car Boot & Stalls
	£'s	£'s	£'s	£'s	£'s	£'s	£'s	£'s	£'s
1981	1,401				759	280			
1982	1,127				586	338			
1983	2,712				97	295	703	1,193	
1984	2,073					146	334	1,555	
1985	701					322			
1986	1,928					384			766
1987	930					319			467
1988	806					223			282
1989	1,610					486			63
1990	1,813					523			263
1991	4,146					353			
1992	1,945					288			677
1993	1,488					332			
1994	5,278			286	843	344			
1995	4,809				323			3,118	28
1996	4,575			224	331			1,792	
1997	5,250			396		549			94
1998	5,706			423		1,002			333
1999	13,327		6,801	1,857	397	1,272			
2000	25,900	17,319	1,126			1,327			

Fund Raising Projects over 20 years

Sponsorship	Dinner Dance	Water Garden / Concerts	Line Dances / Fun Days	Model World / Telethon	Road Shows	Social Events	Duck / Balloon Race	Riverboat Cruises	Quiz	Sundries
£'s	£'s	£'s	£'s	£'s	£'s	£'s	£'s	£'s	£'s	£'s
			253							109
										203
						352				72
										38
						222				157
271						113				394
	100									44
	150									151
	250	575				236				0
	115		555			90				267
	150			1,695	1,497	126				325
	200		280			272				228
	0				416	220				520
	565				848	163	1,248	724		257
	200				421	287		410		22
177	245				249	137		748		672
642	120	1,505				505	928	469		42
229	0		859		747	354		696	325	738
152	288				1,042			602	237	679
1,081	205		258	2,457	1,277			502	218	130

Fund-raising moved onto the Internet in 1998 when we "acquired" the match ball from the game when Southampton thrashed Manchester United by 6 to 3. The auction of this ball on the internet raised £257.78 from a keen local Saints supporter. He was told to bid an unusual price to make sure to win - he did!

Pauline Soper, Head Librarian, has organised many record sales not only to raise funds but also to help move along the many surplus LP's that are kindly donated.

The 1996 great Balloon Race from Ocean Village, released by Adrian Wint, with the winning balloon reaching Italy and almost £1250 raised.

Coins from the Marlands Shopping Centre Fountain make a useful addition to our funds. Although they do need to be washed and dried first. (In the fountain is Darren Jerome, Marlands Manager)

The Army Assault Course at Marchwood helped us to raise thousands of pounds in 1985/86, with "Bertha" in the background.

Collecting Tins at the ready in the Marlands Shopping Centre with Roy Stubbs, Lucy Lockyer and Ken Fielder.

At the front door of Tesco at Christmas.
John Donaldson with his daughters Laura and Rebecca.

CHAPTER 22

Professionalism
1993 to 2002

Geoff Allcock introduced the first element of quality control to the HBA broadcasts by fixing a line from the Toc H studio to his home, in order to monitor the programme output. A GPO line was also connected to the home of Peter Pritchett-Brown the chairman and programme manager.

When the studio was underground everyone worked shoulder to shoulder broadcasting fairly short programmes, with no facilities for presenter training.

The first studio building above ground, had two studios and in the swinging 60's and 70's, along came the DJ's who wanted to play at radio stations. Some members came along, presented their programme, and then went home.

The studio facilities at that time required two engineers and one presenter for each programme, so there were more engineers in our team, which led to programmes being more ambitious, with outside interviews and outdoor adventures being the order of the day.

The Rediffusion wiring system around the Hospitals ceased in the mid 1970's, to be replaced with the hospital's own FM receivers feeding the various new radio programmes that were now available. Radio 1, 2, 3, 4 and Radio Solent gave the hospital patients more choice, but we still maintained the personal touch with our request programmes and with our specialist local programmes.

All the radio programmes are transmitted around the hospitals using FM amplifiers including our own HBA amplifier. Our programmes however were being transported from our studio to our hospital FM amplifiers by means of the GPO (now BT) line network until 1996 when we started broadcasting on our own FM frequency. We now broadcast from the studio transmitter to our FM receivers on the rooftops at the hospitals.

An important feature of our Association has always been our well stocked Library and the incredibly well-organised card index system (and now a computerised index system as well). If our studio building could have a heart it would be the Library. This is the meeting place for all the members to chat and socialise whilst sorting out the music for their programme.

The hard-working librarians, currently led by Pauline Soper find it difficult to keep up with the cataloguing, often interrupted by the "socialising" taking place in their hallowed emporium.

If the Library is the heart, then the blood would be the stock of vinyl and CD's that we own. The collection of long-playing records, all donated, began in the 60's and our selection continues to grow every year. As our listeners are now living longer their memory of "music from their time" is obviously extended and often only available on the old 12" LP's.

The 78's however, had to be discarded when we moved, in 1993, to our new studio, as our modern equipment was not compatible with these wonderful old recordings. We still continued to purchase vinyl 45's until 1998, but CD's have now taken over.

Reel-to-reel tape machines have also become obsolete with the march of technology, and since 1998, electronic editing using minidiscs has taken their place. We still have one tape machine wired up in the studio, so that when required we can play a tape from our archives.

By the time we had arrived in our fourth studio in 1993, the team had moved away from an emphasis on studio engineering, with many other fields of expertise coming to the fore.

Hospital Visiting volunteers actively visit the hospitals to collect requests, but some do not necessarily wish to participate in the programmes, although it has always been a firm understanding that unless you visited the patients and collected requests you would never be "simpatico" to your audience. Unfortunately not every presenter has the spare time to visit the hospitals and present a programme as well.

The outside broadcast team continue producing a regular flow of outdoor live programmes and the Public Address team were increasingly busy, not producing programmes for broadcasting, but actively raising funds.

Presenter-training became a regular feature and not every new applicant survives the auditions. Our programmes are in direct competition with the quality of BBC broadcasting, and it is understood that our presentations and productions must be as good as theirs. In fact our presenters are trained to "speak to the listeners" and not simply to "broadcast to the public" a different, but more personal approach is essential.

The most serious part of the whole organisation now revolved around how we could manage to balance the books. Running costs for our new studios had once again doubled and £16,000 would have to be raised every year, for we have no funding from any Authorities.

It was a difficult decision to employ the services of a cleaning firm but members did not want to polish and vacuum the studio, and this luxury was considered to be a necessity, in order to maintain the fabric of the building and to help with morale.

Members still have to do the washing-up each day - and that is often a battleground - but there are many small jobs our volunteers still do, often without a word of thanks, that must not be left unmentioned. Towels and teatowels are washed every week, milk is regularly purchased, biscuits are sometimes available and important things like stationery, first aid and photocopying seems to appear "free of charge", all helping to keep our costs down.

The annual British Telecom charges was an obvious target for cost savings and broadcasting via an FM frequency was investigated. In 1994 we were quoted a fee of £2,000 per annum for a radio transmission licence. However our engineers persisted down that route and on 1st March 1996 we were granted the frequency of 52.9 Mhz for an annual fee of only £250.

We installed a transmitting aerial on the roof of our studio and receiving aerials on the roof of the General and at the RSH, as fortunately they were "in a straight line" for our private transmitter. This eliminated a significant portion of our BT line circuit network.

The age of the business computer was upon us and small desktop PC's were in almost every home. Radio stations had been computerised since the 80's and our engineers were aware of the sophisticated computers used by the BBC and the Commercial Radio Stations at that time. These were, however, incredibly expensive installations. In 1991 when we were ordering the new studio desks and equipment from MBI, compliments of Tesco's funds, Mel Bowden's factory was constructing a Radio 1 music computer/processor which had a price tag of £100,000. We knew what we would like, but our eyes were far bigger than our pockets.

When we moved into the wonderful new studios it was always the plan to move rapidly towards a 24 hour programme schedule.

Funds were not available, but that had never held HBA back in the past, and ingenuity came to the fore. There was a sustained feed programme called Supergold that broadcast a music programme from 7pm through to 6am, and we were given permission to use this if we needed it.

Our live programmes covered the evenings from 6pm to 10.30pm so all we had to fill was the 6am to 6pm time slot.

Two three-hour videotapes, running on double play filled this slot perfectly. So for the price of two domestic video players, plus a satellite dish to pick up the Sunrise output (a station which relayed IRN), we were on air 24 hours a day.

This was made possible by Tony Harding producing a batch of 6-hour tapes, which incorporated various jingles and promotional messages, so the patient knew it was Hospital Radio on the air.

From September 1994, less than 12 months from our move into our new studio, we were on air 24 hours a day. From 6pm to 10.30pm live, then 10.30pm to 6am on Supergold, followed by 6am to 6pm with our pre-recorded tapes. Yes we were back to taped programmes once again.

This was not ideal and computers were the way forward. Two separate applications were made for Lottery Grants in 1995 and 1996, but failed. Our plans to have computers in each studio were then cut-back to having just one major unit in the control room.

A great deal of research was put in by the executive committee to find the right system for us and, following a visit to Birmingham Hospital Radio to study our selected unit in action, we purchased a Sonifex HDX2000.

We incorporated into our computer system a Satellite Dish connection to IRN (Independent Radio News) and installed our own software, which in total, used £12,000 of our savings.

The 1997 decision to spend so much of our savings on computers was not an easy one for the executive, and one member resigned as he thought this was just "toys for the boys".

Tony Harding, who was between jobs at that time, then spent almost 6 months full-time working in the studio, loading the machine with music and assisting the members with the preparation of their overnight and daytime programmes.

On 6th October 1997, we went live with our own real 24 hour radio service. The live content every evening was still live, but the rest of the 19 hours each weekday was from our computer files. The Satellite Dish brought live IRN news every hour, on the hour, keeping our listeners up to date with current news reports.

Whenever we have a live outside broadcast (football or cricket) during the day, this would switch in, whilst the computer continues running in parallel, but not in transmission mode.

Whilst Tony was busy installing our computerised 24 hour service, the engineers were continuing to add to the facilities that had been originally provided by the Tesco contract.

Talkback was provided to every room in the building and programme monitoring speakers were installed everywhere (even in the toilet - what a cheek!). Televisions were installed and wired into all three studio desks and lights for doorbells and buzzers fitted everywhere, enabling members to be aware of what is going on, whichever room they are in.

From 1st May 1996 we also installed in the control room a video recorder to tape a copy of each day's live programmes. If the Radio Authority wished to check our output, a copy would be available for their inspection. These copies are held for 45 days. This also means that we have a copy of every programme for monitoring the quality of our presenters' performance.

To meet our new financial budgets bigger fund-raising events were required and the members raised £5,278 in 1994 whereas they had only raised £1,488 in 1993. The various fund-raising events can be seen on the separate schedule (chapter 21) highlighting the many money-raising projects in the decades of the 80's and 90's . It was fairly obvious that we were no longer in the "bring and buy sale" mode, and large-scale events had to be undertaken.

This was achieved by organising events in which people outside our membership circle could participate. The Dinner Dances, Socials, Cruises and Line Dances were supported by about 5% of HBA members and 95% from outside supporters.

With a great deal of effort the books were balanced each year throughout the 90's, then we hit the jackpot by getting HBA on to the HSBC charity list. They raised not only the target of £12,000 that we needed to pay for the ISDN line equipment in 2001, but the boys and girls at the Bank, actually raised over £25,000 for us in 1999 and 2000.

We are no longer using the British Telecom analogue lines, which have become obsolete. Incoming live programmes are received using ISDN line connections and outgoing transmissions to the hospitals are broadcast on our private FM waveband.

The old analogue landlines incurred an annual rental fee, with no charges for their usage. The new ISDN system charges are based on usage only, once the installation fee has been paid. Nonetheless these usage charges are fairly significant, particularly with our cricket commentaries lasting all day throughout the summer months.

Professionalism and control of the station is monitored by the monthly Executive Meetings and there are still around 100 members actively involved in our charity. With the station operating efficiently, the only problem of concern is fund-raising and this is no different for any other charity, ways and means must be found to keep us going.

In the year 2052 perhaps there will be a chapter in the 100 year history book showing how the fund-raising problem was resolved. In the meantime the members would do well to look back and reflect on the efforts of Leslie Sullivan and John Stranger, the founders of the football and music sections of our Association, and try to emulate their resourcefulness, by finding a way to overcome our funding problems.

We now have probably the best equipped hospital radio studio in the world, with a 24 hour programme that offers a serious alternative to all the other radio stations.

New members are always welcome to join, but be aware that this is a very exclusive club, and membership is available only to the privileged few who are proud to say they had been invited to be a member of Southampton Hospital Radio.

The 1995 AGM Long Service Awards Ceremony at Anglesea Road Hotel.
Left to right are: Ivor Worsley, Phil Soper, Ken Fielder, Mike Smith, Claire Parsonage, Yvonne Lowe, Graham Fielder, Jane Smith, Graham Lines, Bryan Dowding and Marie Fielder.

When Alan Ball visited the studio it was his birthday so we made a cake. With her arm on his shoulder is his mother watching over him.
Left to right in the studio to celebrate his visit were: Roy Stubbs, Mrs Ball, Amanda Parker, Gary Parker, Sue Dumont, Pauline Soper and Simon Mewett.

A gathering of the clan in March 1998.
Left to right: Ivor Worsley, Jan Dale, Phil Soper, Joan Worsley, Jim Dale, Simon Mewett, Elizabeth Bryant, Roy Stubbs, Ken Holloway, Graham Fielder, Alan Lambourn, Phillip Rioch, Jane Smith, Graham Lines, Ken Fielder, Mike Smith, Bob Crates and Pat Crates.

Our team of Librarians in November 1993 (just before our final move).
Left to right, Joan Worsley, Pauline Soper, Elizabeth Bryant (chief librarian - front),
Margaret Springett, John Springett, June Heard and Kym Bradley.
(Photograph courtesy of Adrian Good)

Ivor Worsley (83), taking tea at the Mayors Parlour with Roy Stubbs. Ivor was honoured
on this day with a special award for his many years of voluntary services, not only to HBA,
but also to The Southampton Talking Echo. (He let it slip that he also worked one day a
week at "Tools for Self Reliance" a charity refurbishing tools for African countries.)
This Annual Ceremony, awarding certificates to exceptional volunteers, is organised by the
local umbrella charity, Southampton Voluntary Services, where Roy is the chairman.

In January 1994 Alan Ball buried a TIME CAPSULE outside the new studio. Gary Parker, Simon Mewett and Amanda Parker can be seen in the background and Roy Stubbs, broadcasting the event, keeps the rain off Alan's shoulders, whilst he worked the shovel. The other young lads in the picture are Saints supporters to whom a drop of rain means nothing.

The "Friday Fun Show" in 1990 left to right Tony Harding, Paul Duell, Clive Shutler, Steve Mullane, Jennifer Wint, Andrew Kennesion, Graham Barber, Chris Pointer, Lesley Canvin, Brian Laurence and Mark Bowen.
One of the more "creative and interactive" shows, where they played lots of fun and games including radio bingo with a huge team of presenters who not only handed out the bingo tickets to the patients, but also delivered the prizes to the winners on the wards.

Members at the AGM
26th March 2002

Back row left to right:

Alison Henderson, Martin Ingoe, Nuala King, Lisa Ford, Pauline Soper.

Ken Holloway, Roy Pickard, Neil Harvey, Alan Lambourn, Yvonne Lowe, James Henley, Bob Tate, Robin Colborne, Carolyn Blake, Paul Duell

Tony Harding, Brian Walker, Christina Bath, Alan Fitch, John Donaldson

Ken Fielder, Ken Flood, Roy Stubbs, Bryony Banger, Philip Day, Rob Davis

Bryan Dowding, Jonathan Newell, Steve Mullane, Marie Fielder, Andrew Barnes

APPENDIX A
Annual Figures (£'s)

Year:	British Telecom Charges	Public Address Income	Public Address Expenses
1981	4,758	55	0
1982	4,512	25	0
1983	5,286	173	0
1984	5,852	450	204
1985	5,060	530	238
1986	5,090	1,954	622
1987	4,375	1,954	646
1988	4,954	2,705	431
1989	4,030	4,075	492
1990	5,011	4,908	925
1991	5,522	4,790	1,328
1992	5,805	5,595	1,487
1993	5,435	6,660	2,289
1994	5,797	8,524	1,869
1995	4,991	7,905	1,125
1996	5,102	7,300	906
1997	4,165	6,715	2,827
1998	3,288	6,005	1,482
1999	3,460	7,265	2,549
2000	3,534	4,755	1,165
20 Year Totals	**96,027**	**82,343**	**20,585**

APPENDIX B

Programme Schedule for 2002

MONDAY

6.00am Southampton AM
Start your day in a dreamy mood when you wake up with Alina Jenkins every weekday morning

9.00am Morning Melodies
Begin the week with Steve Burks for three hours of the best in the middle of the road music, including three in a row at 11am. Plenty of chit chat to entertain you through to midday

Noon Midday Spin
Carolyn Blake will be spinning the discs from the 70's, 80's and 90's all with an upbeat tempo.

2.00pm Afternoon Delight
Light music to delight everyone with Rob Colborne to keep you company.

4.00pm Music Plus
Tony Harding brings you interesting topics from around the world as well as the 60's and 70's music

6.00pm Back Tracks
Steve Burks will play some of the oldies but the music is still high in popularity even today.

7.00pm Jazz and Swingtime
with Roy Pickard, this weeks selection of Big Band sounds and light Jazz Numbers for everyone to enjoy.

7.45pm The Classical Programme
Creating pictures and painting images with music centuries old but still sounding as fresh as the day they were composed.

8.30pm Requestline
In case you have missed the Hospital Visitors, please call our studio on 023 8078 5151 for a request for yourself or for a friend in the next bed.

9.30pm The Other Side of the Bed
Mark Bowen and Theresa Godwin play music for the staff working on the wards as requested by the patients. Don't miss them when they call to collect the requests.

10.30pm to 6.00am HBA Supergold
Music to keep you company through the night with Simon Carter.

TUESDAY

6.00am Southampton AM

Wake up with Alina Jenkins, no need to dress for her, a smile is all you need. She likes you just the way you are.

9.00am Morning Melodies

Steve Burks with the best in music and conversation. At 10am Poet's Corner and at 11am Tuesday's featured CD

Noon Midday Spin

Make a lunch date with Carolyn Blake. Her diet of music and chat is guaranteed to keep you slim

2.00 Afternoon Delight

Rob Colborne with gentle sounds for the afternoon lazy period

4.00 Music Plus

60's and 70's music with a little bit of chat and information from Tony Harding

6.00pm Martin's World of Music

Martin Ingoe with an eclectic mix of music (it means he could not think of a simple format for the programme)

7.00pm Roundabout

Roy Stubbs presents the major interview of the week, where the guests play their own musical selection - a bit like a mixture of Desert Island Discs and an interview with Parkinson.

7.45pm The Tuesday Experience

Lisa Billard and Nuala King. "The latest gossip about the Stars - don't miss this experience"

8.30pm Requestline

Vanessa Naylor is in control. She will be visiting the wards around 6.30pm to collect the requests and messages - look out for her on your ward.

9.30pm Musak for Pleasure

Robert Charles brings you his choice of popular music alongside light comedy and satire

10.30pm to 6am HBA Supergold

Simon Carter plays the hits from the past 40 years for those who cannot sleep. Remember to use your headphones so you do not disturb your neighbours.

WEDNESDAY

6.00am Southampton AM

Easy listening with Alina Jenkins. Great music to start the day off, all you need to join is a smile.

9.00am Morning Melodies

For the very best in light entertainment, at 10am music from the Shows and 11am three in a row, blended superbly by Steve Burks

Noon Midday Spin

Carolyn Blake bringing you music from the latest video releases and news of events which occurred on this day in years gone by, plus upbeat music to fill in the spaces between the reports.

2.00pm Afternoon Delight
Rob Colborne with MOR music plus news and facts of a "Country of the Day"

4.00pm Music Plus
Tony Harding will be spinning music from the 60's and 70's plus showbiz comments from around the world.

6.00pm For the Children
Yvonne Lowe visits the Children's Wards at the General Hospital and plays the children's own choice of music from Postman Pat to the top 20, depending on the age of the listeners. Adults are allowed to tune in but must keep quiet.

7.45pm Karen's Classics

Karen Steele has a light classical touch - her classical music selection is similar. Nothing too heavy is allowed

8.30pm Requestline
Your special programme helping you to keep in touch with your friends and relatives who have called or sent in their requests.

9.30 Recorded Delivery
Jim Adam will be playing something very special for the

mums and mums-to-be in the Maternity Unit at Princess Anne

10.30pm to 6am HBA Supergold
Simon Carter keeping you company through the wee small hours - but mainly seamless music to help you doze.

THURSDAY

6.00am Southampton AM
Start your day the HBA way with Alina Jenkins - there's no better way.

9.00am Morning Melodies
Music from Ruby Murray to Ella Fitzgerald, definitely no Madness or Madonna. Steve Burks entertains you with the best in light musical entertainment. Oh! and plenty of conversation too!

Noon Midday Spin
Two hours with Carolyn Blake to keep the mood in an upbeat tempo through your lunch break.

2.00pm Afternoon Delight
Rob Colborne and delightful music for the hazy, lazy, afternoon shift.

4.00pm Music Plus
Current affairs plus music from the 60's and 70's with Tony Harding in control

6.00pm Musing with Mullane
Steve Mullane with some of his musing(and sometimes amusing) thoughts and some really good music as well.

7.00pm Guy Dunbar's Lounge

Mixing Soul, Sixties, Jazz and Film and TV themes in his own inimitable style.

7.45pm Grande Fromage

Tim Cole with reviews, music and humour.

8.30pm Requestline

If you missed Ron Woodcott when he called to collect requests, please ring our number for your own record choice and Ron will play it for you.

9.30pm Thursday Magazine

Paul Duell is the editor helped by assistants Sarah Tate and Robin Arnold, playing music from the 60's 70's and 80's and reporting on the financial news and comedy items.

10.30pm to 6am HBA Supergold

Simon Carter keeps the music spinning all through the night - for those who cannot nod off.

FRIDAY

6.00am Southampton AM

Ease into the day with Alina Jenkins keeping you company over those first few early morning hours

9.00am Morning Melodies

Almost the weekend and to make the transition easier join Steve Burks for the best in light music and conversation. Friday's featured CD is scheduled to be played at 10am and "three in a row" at 11am.

Noon Midday Spin

If you need an uplifting experience join Carolyn Blake who will be spinning the discs from the 70's, 80's and 90's.

2.00pm Afternoon Delight

Enjoy the company of Rob Colborne with his selection of music through the afternoon

4.00pm Music Plus

Music from the 60's and 70's plus Tony Harding and guest interviews with personalities from around the world of showbiz

6.00pm Friday at Six

The programme title tells you where and when and Tony Harding and Martin Ingoe bring you up-to-date with the latest news from the past week and what to look for over the weekend sports fixtures and events

7.00pm Friday Guide

Good modern music with the occasional oddball. Tune in and enjoy the company of Tracy Warren who will be taking a lighthearted look at next week's daytime TV programmes

7.45pm That's Entertainment

Simon Hobbs reviews the entertainment scene for the happier days ahead when you are able to leave the hospital

8.30pm Requestline
023 8078 5151 is the number to call if you would like us to play your own special request. Steve Burks will be in the studio playing the records and taking your calls

9.30pm Friday Funshow
Sixty minutes of fun with Mark Bowen and Darren Long. They even play "Radio Bingo" so watch out for them visiting the wards in the early evening, to hand out the bingo tickets - you could even win a prize!

10.30pm to 6am HBA Supergold
Music to keep you company through the long nights when you can't sleep, with Simon Carter at the control desk.

SATURDAY

6.00am Southampton AM
On the early morning shift Mark Bowen and Darren Long will help you start your day with a smile.

9.00am Morning melodies
You could be in the garden, tending to the weeds but this is a good alternative. Roy Stubbs plays smooth music all morning and it is guaranteed not to give you a backache.

Noon The Roll Back Hour
No hip hop, no rap, no Spice Girls but lots of hits from the 60's and 70's brought to you by Ray Blow

1.00pm Saturday Club
Our mature presenter with some young friends helping out. This is the second programme devoted personally to all the children in the Children's Wards at the Southampton General - but you can tune in to the fun and games as well if you like.

2.45pm to 5pm Saints at Home - live from their new stadium
Bryan Dowding, Ken Flood and Ken Fielder will supply the live commentary of the 90 minutes play - just as they have been doing for the past 30 years. Hospital radio have relayed every home match since our association was formed in 1952

5.00pm The Saturday Jukebox
Jim Adam with 120 minutes of music selected from his old 45rpm discs interrupted at 5.30pm for Classified Football Results and Pools news

7.00pm That was the year
Hits and news from a year gone by with Alina Jenkins

8.00pm Raise a Smile
Comedy classics from the radio archives

8.30pm Requestline
This is the time your calls would be welcome so that we can play your own special choice of music - the number to ring is 8078 5151

10pm HBA Supergold

Keeping you company through the night with Simon Carter playing continuous smooth music

SUNDAY

6.00am Southampton AM

A little light music will help you to start the day and bring on a warm glow for the early starters

9.00am Morning Melodies

Introduced each Sunday morning by Alan Lambourn. Famous composers and anecdotes surrounding some of the most dramatic pieces from his classical repertoire. The music at times feels as if the paint is still wet

Noon Midday Spin

Andy Barnes brings his own special chatter and music to keep you company through your Sunday lunch break

2.00pm Peanuts and Diamonds

Steve Mullane and Mel Clarke are in the studio each Sunday afternoon and on their "Linkline" spot you could be linking up with your relatives or friends on the telephone in any part of the world. It's a little bit like Surprise Surprise BUT it needs someone to set it up. All you need to do is to contact Steve or Mel on 8078 5151 to make the arrangements. We've been to Malta, America, India and Australia as well as just around the corner to Shirley.

4.00pm Sunday Groove

If you want to be with it, you will need to tune in to the groovy selection played here every Sunday afternoon.

6.00pm Country Bandwagon

Sixty minutes of the best country music you have ever heard - produced and presented by Brian White

7.00pm Melody Time

Rob Colborne will be playing some melodies that will go on forever. You will remember the tune even if you can't remember the title.

8.00pm It's Sunday

Thirty minutes of music and chat with John Donaldson and his special Sunday evening guest

8.30pm Requestline

Carolyn Blake will be calling around the wards and playing requests just for you - if you miss her visit please call 8078 5151 and ask her to play your own personal choice

10.00pm to 6.00am HBA Supergold

At the end of the week you need to start thinking about the week ahead. Simon Carter will keep you company and play continuous music while you think about all the decorating and gardening jobs at home that need your attention.

APPENDIX C
Chairmen

Arthur Leslie Sullivan who created Southampton Hospital Broadcasting must be assumed to be the first chairman, but as there were never any committee meetings, he was a committee of one and did not need a title.

When he joined the music section he became the Honorary Appeals Officer and Fund-raiser, an absolutely vital ingredient to this new part of our charity.

When John Stranger formed the "Music Committee" in 1963, he became the first appointed chairman. John was an efficient manager and his special ability was to recruit and co-ordinate experts. He ran the organisation for seven years, setting-up our first studio and overseeing the move into the second one. A promotion in the business world meant John had to move away from Southampton and it was a sad day for the Association when he left in 1970.

Peter Maggs, who had just retired from his role as Producer in charge of BBC South, took over as the acting chairman when John Stranger left. However he then began a lecturing position at the College of Technology, which distracted him from HBA problems.

In early 1971 the members, at the AGM, appointed Peter Pritchett-Brown who had been the programme controller for a few years. Peter's day job was as Presentation Director at the Southern Television studios. Peter continued in his HBA role as programme controller as well as being the chairman, monitoring our programmes from his home via a GPO line connection, to speakers in his front room.

Allan St John Holt held various administrative and fund-raising jobs and was for many years, in charge of "waste paper". He was promoted to the chairman's role in 1979, when Peter's day job demanded more of his time. Allan steered the Association through the move from the Bassett studio centre to the new Chest Hospital studio. Unfortunately Allan's own business commitments dragged him away from HBA in 1982.

Ron Fitton, a marketing expert, was elected as the chairman for three years until 1985 when he handed over to Bryan Dowding. Bryan had been a member of HBA since 1969 working in various administrative jobs and also as part of the football commentating team. He reported not only on the Saints local matches, but also travelled to many of the away games when the Saints team were performing miracles and winning glittering prizes.

Bryan had volunteered to take on the chairman's job for only three years and he handed over to John Challis in 1988. John had been the Treasurer at HBA since 1971 and moved into the chair on his retirement from the NatWest Bank. He had been the HBA bank manager for over 20 years and helped to keep us in the black the whole time.

He vacated the chair due to ill health after a couple of years and I took over in 1991, a position I have now enjoyed for more than 11 years.

In the daytime I am an accountant and bring to the executive a degree of financial reporting and control not present before. The monthly Treasurer's Report became a monthly profit and loss account, setting the actual results for the month, against a budget.

At first the executive members were not too enthusiastic about such accounting numbers, but after a couple of years they began to criticise in some detail if things were not going according to budget. An excellent way to monitor and run a business. I have been told off that "We are not a business, we are a charity" - nonetheless I believe that similar monthly controls are just as important.

A presenter since 1981 and a "performer" on many public address events over the years, public relations, financial control and fund-raising, have been my chosen fields in which to help HBA. I have also been fortunate in being able to use my Tuesday evening chat show "Roundabout" to promote HBA to the many and varied supporters of our cause.

It has been said that "It will cost you a fortune to be a guest on Roy's Show", however I have found no better way of convincing anyone of the merits of our service, once they have seen our magnificent studios and taken part in a broadcast. I always give them a cassette recording of their programme and this is all the thanks they need. (I then ask for money!)

Looking forward, I am trying to extend the Patientline service to the areas not at present covered, improve on our distribution system in order to reach out to the Old People's Homes, Nursing Homes and other Hospitals in Southampton, whilst at the same time, constantly updating the studio equipment and systems, in order to keep up with modern technology.

The length of service as highlighted in the current member's list (Appendix D), shows the long-term commitment given by the members, and it has been an honour to work with such a wonderful group of like-minded friends for such a long time.

APPENDIX D

Lists of Members

From the daily broadcasting log records I have extracted members' names and listed them in alphabetical order.

Instead of scheduling each and every one of the 27 years from 1966 to 2002, where these records are available, I have selected every five years as a snapshot.

With apologies to any members who may have been missed out because they may have joined and left between these five year samples.

Also sincere apologies to the members involved in the outside broadcast and public address teams and to the many hospital visitors whose names will have been missed. There were probably some Librarians and Engineers who have also been missed.

As many of these member's names have not been recorded in the broadcasting log books, regretfully it has not been possible to recognise everyone on these lists.

However I have also reviewed Yvonne's membership records to try to capture some of the "missing persons" and wherever possible I have added them to the nearest relevant year when they were a member.

On the final schedule dated January 2002 I have recorded the members, not in alphabetical order, but in date order when they were officially appointed as a member. Actually most members were active in the Association for a few months before their official joining date.

It is interesting to note that in the 2002 list almost half of the membership have been in the Association for over 10 years.

List of Members - 1966

Geoff Allcock
Stuart Allcock
Len Aldridge
Robert Ashbolt
J. Averson
Jim Barnes
Elaine Barnes
Roger Blanchford
Derek Brandon
Mary Carlton
Derek Chant
Janet Clark
George Clogg
Dr Edwin Course
Margaret Cooper
R.J.Davies
Dennis Dexter
Jean Dixon
Frank Le Druillenec
Johnny Dymond
Colin Edge
Christine Elgar
Gerald Farmer
Ken Flood
Peter Fry
Guy Garrett

Genie Garrett
Sonya Garrett
John Gibbons
Ann Gibbons
Ray Green
Paul Headland
Monica Hinves
Jim Holmes
Marie Hudson
Brian Jameson
Larry Kaye
Alan Lambourn
Roger Large
Rosemary Lee
G Mainward
Ralph Mason
Jeremy Maynard
Zena Millard
B.Miller-Smith
Eddie Munford
Roger Munford
Judy Munford
V. Pearce
Carole Phillips
Frank Phillips
Trevor Price

Anita Richards
Charles Richards
Colin Rudd
John Russell
David Shepperd
Paul Shoosmith
Peter Simpkin
Carole Stone
Dallas Stone
Frank Staight
John Stranger
Maureen Stranger
Leslie Sullivan
Marjorie Sullivan
Peter Tanner
Peter Trott
John Walker
Ian Ward
J. Weber
Barry West
Robin Wheatcroft
M. Whitington
David Williams
Marie Louise Woodman
Jill Zebedee

List of Members - 1969

Geoff Allcock
Stuart Allcock
Alan Barnes
Jim Barnes
Alexandra Bejda
Michael Birkett
Graham Board
Sue Bodger
Derek Brandon
Bob Brown
John Paddy Brown
Ronnie Burns
David Caldwell
Andrew Campbell
Cathy Churcher
Nigel Clough
Dr Edwin Course
Martin Dale
Dennis Dexter
Frank Le Druillenec
Johnny Dymond
Jim Elliott
Keith Elliott(snr)
Keith Elliott(Jnr)
T. Evans
Ken Fielder
Graham Fielder
Ken Flood
Steve Frampton

Brian Frost
Guy Garrett
Genie Garrett
Sonya Garrett
John Gibbons
M. Green
Paul Headland
Bob Heather
Mervyn Hodkinson
Jack Horner
Geoff Hunkin
Barrie Jackson
Clive Jacobs
Alan Lambourn
Roger Large
Graham Lines
Chris Litton
John Lloyd
Ralph Mason
Jeremy Maynard
George McGreavey
Zena Millard
Shirley Morgan
Ray Moore
Peter Moseley
Eddie Munford
Roger Munford
Don Ozmond
Frank Phillips

Diane Philpott
Stuart Powell
Trevor Price
Anita Richards
Aliki Rogers
Nicky Rogers
Alan Ross
Johnny Russell
Richard Russell
Paul Shoosmith
Peter Simpkin
Andrew Slee
Chris Smith
Kathleen Stone
Dallas Stone
John Stranger
Maureen Stranger
Leslie Sullivan
Marjorie Sullivan
Jane Teare
Ian Ward
Barry West
Robin Wheatcroft
Paul Wilkinson
Mary Wood
Lloyd Woodland

List of Members - 1973

Geoff Allcock
Stuart Allcock
Marie Ashley-Smith
Brian Ault
Jane Baron
Alexandra Bejda
Simon Bliss
Barbara Bond
Peter Boothby
Marie Bostock
Mark Bowen (No.1)
Peter Pritchett-Brown
Keith Butler
Roger Butterfield
Margaret Callan
Ivan Champion
Nigel Crewe
Helen Cox
Martin Dale
Sonya Delamere
Bryan Dowding
B. Dutt
Jim Emery
Phillip Farlowe
Colin Fay
Ken Fielder
Graham Fielder
Ken Flood
Guy Garrett

John Gibbons
Brian Godwin
Geoffrey Grandy
Nick Green
John Grove
Heather Gunton
Robin Hamilton
Anthony Harding
Bob Heather
Lynn Hitchcock
Mervyn Hodkinson
Geoff Hodkinson
Stephen Holder
Allan St. John Holt
Norman Hutchison
Barrie Jackson
Clive Jacobs
Clive John
Robin Kay
Alan Lambourn
Graham Lines
Chris Litton
Ian Livesey
Tim Marshall
Phillip Molyneux
Chris Moody
Eddie Munford
Andy Newton

Eric Robinson
Pat Scriven
Paul Shoosmith
Peter Simpkin
Andrew Slee
Chris Smith
Helen Staples
Richard Steele
Dallas Stone
Leslie Sullivan
Marjorie Sullivan
Ashley Sutton
Eric Thompson
Sheila Tracy
Ann Tupper
Martyn Tupper
June Tytherleigh
Bill Walker
Ian Ward
John Watkin
Lesley Wellman
Stewart White
Liz Whitney
Nora Williams
Gwen Willis
David Wisdom
A. Woodrow
Ivor Worsley

List of Members - 1978

Val Ash
Brian Ault
Jane Ault
Nicki Baker
Jane Baron
David Bellam
Mark Bowen (No.1)
Colin Briggs
Jonathan Capel
Richard Clegg
Julie Cottam
David Cross
James Dale
Janice Dale
Gill Davis
Mike Dennis
Bryan Dowding
David Doling
Richard Ellis
Gwladys Evans
Ken Fielder
Graham Fielder
Marie Fielder
Ken Flood

Paul Freedman
Barbara Garrett
Ken Gladstone-Millar
Peter Godfrey
John Guille
Paulette Hampton
Anthony Harding
Peter Hawken
Ken Holloway
Dominic Horne
Barrie Jackson
Joan Johnson
Ray Johnson
Elizabeth Kinloch
Ian King
Alan Lambourn
Graham Lines
Chris Litton
Yvonne Lowe
Patrick Lunt
Lee McKenzie
Jane Mosedale
Eddie Munford
Derek Petty

Peter Phillips
Keith Punt
John Poxon
Tony Rees
Chris Riddett
Eric Robinson
Claire Rowthorne
Paul Shoosmith
Gareth Sims
Kevin Sims
Michael Smith
Steve Smith
Pat Smith
Phillip Smith
Phil Soper
Robin Thomas
Ann Tupper
Martyn Tupper
John Waldron
Lesley Wellman
Barry West (No.2)
Malcolm Wright
Ivor Worsley
John Young

List of Members - 1983

Val Ash
Nigel Ashton
Trudi Barber
Jane Baron
Sue Bergin
Peter Berry
Christine Berry
Mark Bowen (No.1)
Colin Briggs
Paul Canning
Mike Castle
Phillipa Colton
Andrew Coote
James Dale
Janice Dale
Mike Dennis
Bryan Dowding
Bob Elliott
Gwladys Evans
Bob Everitt
Ron Fitton
Steve Feeney
Ken Fielder
Graham Fielder
Marie Fielder
Simon Fish
Ken Flood
Paula Fower
Richard Franklin
Ken Gladstone-Millar

Dorothy Guyatt
Anthony Harding
Ken Holloway
Debbie House
Keith House
Trevor Humphrey
Ian Hunt
Madeleine Jennings
Hazel Jones
Andy Judd
Elizabeth Kinloch
Tony Knight
Irene Lamb
Tracy Lambert
Dorothy Lambert
Leonard Lambert
Alan Lambourn
Trudy Large
Ken LeLievre
Graham Lines
Chris Litton
Yvonne Lowe
Michael Lynch
Andrew McKenna
Chris Moody
Lee Moulsdale
Eddie Munford
Pat Murray
Julie Murray
Suzanne O'Shea

Derek Petty
Peter Phillips
Mark Powell
Graham Rawlings
Tony Rees
Chris Riddett
Phillip Rioch
Eric Robinson
Claire Rowthorne
Paul Rudd
Colin Ryde
Claire Salter
Tony Seaton
Thomas Selby
William Shaw
Patrick Shea
Paul Shoosmith
Tony Sinfield
Michael Smith
Chris Smith
Phil Soper
Steve Spacagna
Roy Stubbs
Sharon Tate
Mike Tiller
Libby Viener
Julia Wheatland
Christine Whent
Derek Wise
Ivor Worsley

List of Members - 1988

Val Ash	Colin Corcoran	Paul Gunston
Perry Baker	K Corcoran	Anthony Harding
Jane Baron	John Cornforth	Cheryl Harding
Terence Barter	Fiona Crust	Chris Harding
Andrew Bellows	James Dale	Alia Hassan
Simon Bennett	Janice Dale	June Heard
Peter Berry	Mike Dennis	Julia Heard
Jason Bevis	Adrian Denny	Terry Henderson
Martyn Bignell	Nicholas Dermody	Simon Hobbs
Louise Bowden	Bryan Dowding	Ken Holloway
Mark Bowen (No.2)	Paul Duell	Henry Howell
Graham Bowring	Phillip Eldridge	Julie Imeson
Stuart Britton	Gwladys Evans	Paul James
Norma Campbell	Peter Fellbrich	Harriman James
Dean Cannard	Ron Fitton	Lynne Jenkins
Paul Canning	Ken Fielder	Steve Jenkins
Teresa Carlins	Graham Fielder	Sheila Jones
Nick Carroll	Marie Fielder	Alan Jones
Mike Castle	Ken Flood	John Jordan
Clare Castle	Richard Franklin	Simon Jury
Jonathan Chapman	Simon Fry	Mary Jury
Glenda Charles	Max Gillibrand	Jeremy Kapp
Suzanne Christian	Ken Gladstone-Millar	Elizabeth Kinloch
Ray Clancey	Georgina Glover	Susie Kirsten
Ian Coombs	David Grigg	Alan Lambourn
Deanne Coombs	Kerry Gunner	Andrew Lane

List of Members - 1988 (contd.)

Brian Laurence
Hugh Lawson
Ken LeLievre
Graham Lines
Chris Litton
Yvonne Lowe
Alison Manning
Cher McInness
Peter McNaught
Scott Mills
Dennis Mitchell
Eric Moore
Lee Moulsdale
Steve Mullane
Eddie Munford
Pat Murray
Julie Murray
Andrew Pearman
Chris Pointer
Joan Radley
Patricia Rees
Michael Reed
Martin Ridley
Phillip Rioch
Eric Robinson
Ann Robinson

Peter Rouse
Claire Rowthorne
Colin Ryde
Diane Saunders
W E Saunders
Patrick Shea
Tony Simpson
Paul Shoosmith
Susan Slinn
Kate Smart
Fiona Smith
William Smith
Michael Smith
Laurie Socker
Phil Soper
Pauline Soper
B L Southcott
Jon Spooner
Karen Steel
Helen Street
Roy Stubbs
J J Sutcliffe
Christopher Terry
Michael Thomas
Donald Udall
Roger Vicarage

Bruce Wade
Helen Walker
Stephen Walker
Robert Wallace
Martin West
Nick West
Jacqueline Weston
Barry White
Heather White
David White
Jayne Whitelock
Paul Wignall
Elizabeth Williams
Jenny Williams
Derek Wise
Roy Woodcock
Nigel Woodcock
Ann Woodham
Peter Woods
Mark Woodward
Phillip Woodward
Heather Wootten
Ivor Worsley
Joan Worsley
Steve Wright
John Young

List of Members - 1993

Pauline Adams
George Adamson
Val Ash
Graham Barber
Andrew Barnes
Graham Barnes
Peter Barnes
Jane Baron
Willem deBeer
Richard Bentley
Glynis Biggs
John Biles
Carolyn Blake
Mark Bowen (No.2)
Kym Bradley
Stuart Britton
Elizabeth Bryant
Lesley Canvin
Mike Castle
Ian Chapman
Martin Chantler
Sheila Clark
Neil Critchlow
Dorota Dabrowska
James Dale
Janice Dale
Robin Day
Robert Day

Mark Diaper
Bryan Dowding
Paul Duell
Susan Dumont
Wendy Dumper
Martine Dunn
Tracey Edwards
Ken Fielder
Graham Fielder
Marie Fielder
Alan Fitch
Ken Flood
Ken Gladstone-Millar
Adrian Good
John Greenstreet
Richard Hamilton
Anthony Harding
Chris Hardy
Colm Harrisson
Emma Harvey
Karen Harvey
June Heard
William Heller
Steve Hicks
Kevin Hillier
Jonathan Hills
Simon Hobbs
Douglas Hobbs

Ken Holloway
Andrew Hoyle
Sandra Ingram
Paul James
Nick Janaway
Natalie Jaque
Sarah Jones
Simon Jury
Andrew Kennesion
Andrew Ketchley
Emma Kinchenton
Paula Kingsnorth
Alan Lambourn
David Lawes
Chris Lee
Ken LeLievre
Graham Lines
Paul Littfield
Chris Litton
Maria Lock
Sarah Locke
Angela Logan
Yvonne Lowe
Rosie McGiveron
Charlotte McLeod
Sandra McLoud
Simon Mewett
Jennifer Mitchell

List of Members - 1993 (contd.)

Derek Mitchell
Julian Mitchell
Doreen Moger
Eric Moore
James Moore
Richard Moormay
Alison Morgan
Andy Moseby
Andrew Mosley
Steve Mullane
Eddie Munford
Linda Murphy
Jonathan Newell
Roy Newport
Timothy Northover
Chris Noon
Francis Pacifico
Gary Parker
Alex Perry
Chris Pointer
Bruce Pomeroy
Troy Power
Phillip Prior
Nigel Pugh
Alan Purvis
Juliette Quinney
Lee Rawlings
Phillip Rioch

Eric Robinson
Lucinda Roch
John Rodgers
Lucinda Rook
Claire Rowthorne
Michael Sams
Alan Seabrook
James Selwood
Angela Sharma
Joan Sharpe
Paul Shoosmith
Clive Shutler
Annette Simon
Nicholas Simons
Annette Simonson
Paula Simpson
Mathew Simmonds
Kim Skinner
Michael Smith
Phil Soper
Pauline Soper
Doug Spade
John Springett
Karen Steel
Helen Street
Roy Stubbs
Robert Tate
Sarah Tate

Simon Tilley
John Tipper
Helen Walker
Simon Waller
Mike Ward
Michael Wardrop
Stephanie Warren
Tracey Warren
Jean Weavers
Alan Welch
Amanda West
Tony West
Marianne Westcott
Martin White
Lovett Whitelaw
Alison Wilson
Emma Wilson
Carolyn Wing
Helen Winsborough
Adrian Wint
Derek Wise
Mark Woodward
Ivor Worsley
Joan Worsley
Steve Wright
John Young

List of Members - 1998

Maria Aldworth	Robin Colborne	Emma Golby-Kirk
Corinna Allen	Heather Cosser	Anthony Harding
Joanne Arnold	Sarah Dakin	Lorraine Hawthorne
Robin Arnold	James Dale	June Heard
Louise Atkinson	Janice Dale	Lucy Heatlie
Mark Austin	Timothy Dale	Alison Henderson
Noel Bachman	Mathew Danahar	Ryan Hewitt
Graham Barber	Bryan Dowding	Simon Hobbs
Andrew Barnes	Paul Duell	Ken Holloway
Lynsey Bartlett	Susan Dumont	Linda Husband
Jane Baron	Lawrence Du Pavey	Martin Ingoe
Christina Bath	Max Eaves	Alina Jenkins
Kate Belcher	Alec Elliott	Nigel Jones
Alison Bell	Clare Espline	Jonathan Kaye
Martin Bennett	Steve Evans	Andrew Kennesion
Lisa Billard	Ken Fielder	Nigel King
Carolyn Blake	Graham Fielder	Alan Lambourn
Raymond Blow	Marie Fielder	Mathew Lancey
Steve Boston	Alan Fitch	Tony Lascelles
Mark Bowen (No.2)	Paul Fitzgerald	Nicholas Layton
Stuart Britton	Adrian Flavell	Kwi-Chang Lee
Elizabeth Bryant	Ken Flood	Ken LeLievre
Steve Burks	Alan Galpin	Graham Lines
Anthony Butler	Janet Glackin	Chris Litton
Hermina Campbell	Ken Gladstone-Millar	Maria Lock
Mike Castle	Mathew Goddard	Joseph Lockyer
Bethany Chilvers	Martin Goddard	Lucy Lockyer
Mel Clarke	Theresa Godwin	Darren Long

List of Members - 1998 (contd.)

Yvonne Lowe
Ted Mackney
Peter Markey
Florence Mathews
Lucy May
Neil McAuliffe
Robert McGowan
Hanna Meritainen
Simon Mewett
Jane Miller
Lorraine Molloy
Eric Moore
Steve Mullane
Chris Murphy
Natasha Murray
Jonathan Newell
Michael Newport
Chris Noon
Gary Orchard
Graham Othen
Alison Owen
Gary Parker
Amanda Parker
Anne-Marie Parnell
Claire Parsonage
Chris Pointer
Brian Pollock

Bruce Pomeroy
Gary Pompa
Peter Pope
Gary Prescott
Stephen Price
Fraser Richardson
Phillip Rioch
Maria Ritzema
Phillip Rixon
Eric Robinson
Marianne Rosenquist
Emma Rose
Stephen Rush
Barry Ryerson
Alan Seabrook
Richard Sharp
Clive Shutler
Ben Sillifant
Brian Sims
Claire Singleton
Michael Smith
Phil Soper
Pauline Soper
Karen Steel
Helen Stephens
Richard Stockdale
Roy Stubbs

Alex Tame
Robert Tate
Sarah Tate
Steve Tippen
Tracy Turnbull
Lynn Turner
David Virgo
Brian Walker
Mark Walsh
Alexandra Ward
Stephanie Warren
Tracey Warren
Bevis Watts
Ronald Westcott
Benjamin White
Rachel Williams
Suzanne Williams
Stephanie Willson
Adrian Wint
Jennifer Wint
Derek Wise
Natasha Wood
Mark Woodward
Ivor Worsley
Joan Worsley
John Young

List of Members - 2002 (January)

MEMBERSHIP STARTING DATE ORDER

Aug 1958	Kenneth Flood	Oct 1985	Simon Hobbs
June 1964	Alan Lambourn	May 1986	Pauline Soper
June 1967	Kenneth Fielder	June 1986	Eric Robinson
July 1967	Graham Fielder	Sept 1986	Steve Mullane
Mar 1968	Graham Lines	Feb 1987	Paul Duell
Sept 1968	Chris Litton	April 1988	Mark Bowen
Nov 1969	Bryan Dowding	July 1988	Eric Moore
Mar 1971	Marie Fielder	June 1989	Maria Lock
Mar 1972	Jane Smith (Baron)	Mar 1990	Sarah Tate
April 1973	Anthony Harding	Mar 1990	Adrian Wint
July 1973	Ivor Worsley	Mar 1990	Jonathan Newell
Jan 1974	Ken Holloway	April 1991	Bruce Pomeroy
July 1974	James Dale	Feb 1992	Tracy Warren
Mar 1975	Michael Smith	June 1992	Alan Fitch
June 1976	Janice Dale	Oct 1992	Carolyn Blake
Feb 1976	Ken Gladstone-Millar	Oct 1992	Clive Shutler
Mar 1977	Claire Parsonage	Oct 1992	Robert Tate
May 1977	Phil Soper	April 1993	John Young
May 1978	Yvonne Lowe	May 1993	Graham Barber
Aug 1978	Phillip Rioch	Sept 1993	Gary Parker
Aug 1979	Derek Wise	Nov 1993	Andrew Barnes
Feb 1981	Roy Stubbs	Mar 1994	Simon Mewett
Aug 1981	Ken LeLievre	July 1994	Karen Steel
Sept 1984	Chris Pointer	July 1994	Theresa Godwin
Nov 1984	Joan Worsley	July 1994	Joseph Lockyer

List of Members - 2002 (January) - contd.

MEMBERSHIP STARTING DATE ORDER

Aug 1994	Graham Othen	April 1999	John Brodrick
Dec 1994	Nigel Jones	April 1999	Roy Pickard
Feb 1995	Robin Colborne	May 1999	James Adam
Feb 1995	Darren Long	June 1999	Stuart Britton
Oct 1995	Mel Clarke	Sept 1999	Neil Harvey
Oct 1995	Robin Arnold	Oct 1999	Anthony Jordan
Oct 1995	Lorraine Hawthorne	Oct 1999	Holly Barnes-Thomas
Dec 1995	Michael Castle	April 2000	Philip Day
June 1996	Steve Burks	April 2000	Stephen Ireland
Sept 1996	Benjamin White	Aug 2000	Finlay Fraser
Sept 1996	Christine Bath	Nov 2000	Suzanne Harding
Nov 1996	Martin Ingoe	Nov 2000	Darren Collings
Mar 1997	Alex Tame	Jan 2001	Vanessa Naylor
Mar 1997	Linda Husband	Jan 2001	Lisa Jane Ford
July 1997	Chris Murphy	Feb 2001	James Henley
July 1997	Ronald Westcott	April 2001	Erik Pearson
July 1997	Lisa Billard	May 2001	Phillipa Drew
Oct 1997	Alison Henderson	May 2001	Alina Jenkins
Oct 1997	RobertMcGowan	May 2001	Brian White
Oct 1997	Brian Walker	Oct 2001	Bryony Banger
May 1998	Jennifer Wint	Oct 2001	Zoe Cornell
May 1998	Raymond Blow	Oct 2001	Peter Harvey
Aug 1998	Tim Cole	Oct 2001	Jennifer Langridge
April 1999	Nuala King	Nov 2001	Douglas Eltham
April 1999	John Donaldson	Dec 2001	Steven Pothecary